THE MC...

125 years of the Mexborough Montagu Hospital Charity Cup 1897-2022

Words and design: Steven Penny

Research: Chris Brook

Foreword: Dennis Priestley

in association with

First published in Great Britain in 2022

Copyright – Steven Penny 2022

Penny for your Sports Publications

Steven Penny has asserted his right under the Copyright, Designs and Patents Act 1988 to be identified as the author of this work. All rights reserved. No part of this publication may be reproduced, distributed, or transmitted in any form or by any means, including photocopying, recording, or other electronic or mechanical methods, without the prior written permission of the author.

ISBN: 978-1-7392267-0-1

Printed by
Blackwell Print,
Charles Street, Great Yarmouth
Norfolk, NR30 3LA
(*www.blackwellprint.co.uk*)

To offset any greenhouse gases used in the production of this book,
119 trees have been planted and 1,190kg of CO2 offset

steve@stevepennymedia.co.uk

A **Penny** for your **Sports** production

Contents

	Page
Foreword	5
Introduction	9
Family Album	11
Bennett 12	
Burkinshaw. 13	
Billups. 14	
Dawson 14	
Frith 14	
Kerry. 15	
Needham 15	
Oxer 16	
Simon 17	
Smelt. 17	
Smith 18	
Taylor 18	
Watkin. 18	
Watson. 17	
Whitehouse 19	
Wilkinson. 20	
Decades	21
1897-99 21	
1900-09. 23	
1910-19 26	
1920-29 29	
1930-39 32	
1940-49. 35	
1950-59 40	
1960-69. 43	
1970-79 44	
1980-89 47	
1990-99 49	
2000-09 51	
2010-19 53	
2020-22. 56	
Meet at the Mont	60
Trivia	62

(Continued overleaf)

	Page
Players	63

- Kenny Boden 63
- Allan Craw 66
- Mark Crook 66
- Steve Ellor 67
- Jeff Earnshaw 67
- Brian Hill 67
- Kenny King 68
- Harry Newey 69
- Albert Pape 69
- Pete Pettit 69
- Wilf Race 69
- George and Ted Robledo 70
- Tony Rodgers 71
- Arthur Roberts 73
- Jimmy Sansome 73
- Lionel Smith 73
- Rex Trickett 74
- Jamie Williams 74
- The Elite 75

Clubs	77

- Denaby & Cadeby MW 78
- Denaby United 79
- Mexborough Athletic 80
- Manvers Main 81
- Mexborough Main Street 81
- Swinton Athletic 82
- Wombwell Main 83
- AFP 83
- Rawmarsh Welfare 83
- Goldthorpe United 84
- Hickleton Main 84
- Houghton Main 84
- Parkgate Welfare 84

Miscellaneous	85

- Hospital and Comforts Fund . . .86
- Committee 88
- Captains 89
- Referees 90
- Mascots 93
- Publicity 94
- Making history 96
- Web wise 99
- Lest We Forget 109
- Other cups 110
- Subscribers 114
- Final whistle 119

Statistics	100
Acknowledgments	116

Foreword

Dennis Priestley
World Darts Champion
1991 and 1994

Growing up, the Mont was always a part of family life for us and it was an Easter Monday event to go watch the final – still is! It is a true community tradition and it's great that it is still going strong after all these years. It really is embedded in Mexborough folk lore.

I am more associated with a much different sport to football but the Montagu Cup has played a big part in my life – and before I was even thought about! Billy Westwood won the Mont in 1904 with Mexborough Town. He was my mother's dad but died in World War One. My grandma also died young so we have no memorabilia from my grandad's time.

My dad Maurice also played a bit but it was around the time of World War Two. I'm sure he would have played in the Mont. I know my uncle Geoff did. He was with Bowbroom and they had a decent team for many years.

As a kid I was a decent player and captained my school team – Doncaster Road. We played in the Totty Cup but didn't win many games.

I played in the early rounds of the Mont, but was never with a good enough team to reach the final. I turned out for the Miners' Arms and South Yorkshire pubs and also Parkgate Iron & Steel teams before going with Gordon Swann to Golden Smithies – a Manvers Sunday side. I did my knee in there and didn't play again.

Of course, all the funds raised from the Mont goes to a good cause. The Montagu Hospital has played a major part in many people's lives – not least because so many were born there!

I was born at home but my three eldest children – Michael Dennis, Kerry Anne and Wayne Kenneth – were all born in the maternity unit there. It was a grand sounding name but in practice was a couple of old Nissen huts round the back of the main building!

My youngest son Adam Daniel Andrew Maurice was born at Doncaster and it's such a shame that so many of our local hospital facilities have been moved away. At least with the money raised through the Mont for the Comforts Fund, those people in the hospital can be better looked after.

Darts has taken me all over the world but I'm a Mexborough lad through and through and reading this book has brought back so many happy memories, as well as giving me lots of information I never knew about.

I've really enjoyed flicking through this book. It's full of nostalgia and for all those records over the

A knee injury robbed Dennis Priestley of the chance to make his name in the Mont – he didn't do too badly in the darts world instead though!

125 years to be brought together like this is a tribute to the people involved and also those in the past who kept the records.

Many of the players and teams mentioned are ones I grew up with and I am happy to say that lots of them are still around.

The Mont is everything that local sport should be. It gives players with no hope of becoming professionals the chance to be heroes in their own community.

Mindst you, quite a few lads did turn out to be good enough to become pros. A few that I knocked about with as a lad went on to play in the Football League – the likes of Brian Turton, Alan Warboys, Pete Middleton and Geoff Salmons.

I remember when Frank Barlow captained the England Schoolboys team at Wembley against Germany, I was at Adwick Road School and they got a bus up so we could all go and cheer him on.

I hope you enjoy reading this book and being a part of this wonderful competition of ours.

(Editor's note: Dennis' father Maurice played for Royston High Street in the early rounds of the 1937/8 Mont. His uncle, Geoff, scored in the 1951 final, sending the goalkeeper the wrong way with a penalty, but was on the losing side for Bowbroom. He also played for Denaby Rovers in the 1945 televised semi-final, and was a winner with Bowbroom in 1955 and 1958).

LEADING THE WAY THROUGH THE YEARS

As a major employer in South Yorkshire, Stelrad Radiators has continued to invest heavily in its role within its local communities through its support, sponsorship and involvement with and in local sporting and charitable events. The Montagu Cup is a very important one of those that the company has been involved in since 2015, through both its support for the football and for the local hospital. We have seen impressive fundraising exploits through the annual cup competition and cup final that traditionally takes place on Easter Bank Holiday Monday. It's a link that Stelrad is proud of and which is now an important part of the company's annual community activities.

Stelrad Radiators has seen many of its employees involved in local sporting success over the years and several of its employees have featured in the Montagu Cup competition, appearing in the finals over the years, including a few current employees:

Shaun Wilkinson
Winner in 1983 and 1984 with Main Street and 1986 with Swinton Athletic. Runner-up in 1988 with Swinton Athletic.

Chris Watson
Winner in 1987, 1999 and 2000 with Main Street. Runner-up in 1986, 1995 and 1998 with Main Street.

Andy Linacre
Runner-up in 1989 with Saracens.

Steve Johnson
Winner 1986 with Swinton Athletic.

1920s

1929
The Hattersley Brothers make industrial gas boilers and stove-grates in Mexborough.

1930s

1936
The company begins as Steel Radiators Ltd.

1960s

1969
Steel Radiators Ltd merges with Hattersley Brothers, to form Hattersley Stelrad and the company's life as a radiator manufacturer begins.

2022
Stelrad Radiator Group floats on the Stock Exchange and is renamed Stelrad Group plc.

2020
The new 'Home Series' range is launched.

2017
Stelrad.com starts selling online to the general public.

2013
The Vita Series is launched and marketed to one-off installers and homeowners.

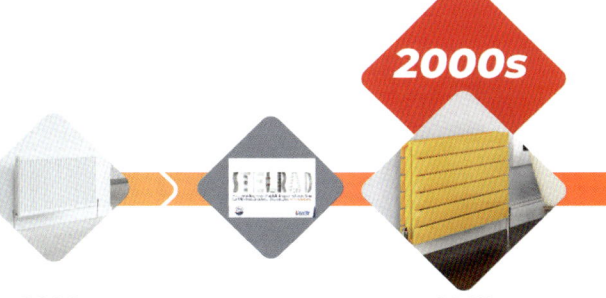

2000
The Stelrad 'Compact Radiator' is launched to replace the 'Accord Compact'.

2003
Component Plant moves towards full automation using an automatic feeding system from hand-fed connections.

2003
The £3.8m National Distribution Centre (NDC) is officially opened by John Healey MP.

1998
The Mexborough site sees a multi-million pound investment to install a fourth high-speed line together with three new helium test facilities and the first Winter convector press.

1994
Stelrad House is built at Mexborough.

1990
The Stelrad 'Accord Radiator' is replaced by the Stelrad 'Elite'.

1971
Hattersley Stelrad is renamed Stelrad Group.

1980
The Stelrad 'Super Radiator' is replaced by the 'Accord Radiator'. The Cold Box Shop is opened for boiler manufacturing.

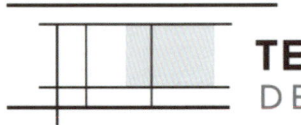

The Mont

The Mexborough Montagu Hospital Cup is played in the Don & Dearne area of South Yorkshire – including Rotherham, Doncaster and Barnsley. This area was the heartland of the South Yorkshire Coalfield and the vast industries that grew up alongside the mines.

The teams who played in the Montagu Cup reflect the history of the area. Wombwell Main were the first of the winners linked to the coal mines, while Mexborough Grand Central Loco were the first railway-based finalists in 1915. Winners soon after World War One were the Swinton Discharged Soldiers and Sailors and after World War Two, Jump Home Guard. Since then, there have been victorious teams representing a variety of organisations, including churches, chemical works, steel works, car manufacturers, as well as clubs and pubs.

For more than 100 of its 125-year history, Montagu Cup finals have been played on the Hampden Road ground. The first was on Easter Monday 1897 and the 2022 125th anniversary final, like many before, was also played there on Easter Monday.

Thousands of people have been involved in the Mont over those 125 years, on and off the field, and it is to those that this book is dedicated.

The book would not have been possible without the support of title sponsors Stelrad Radiators (see Pages 6, 7 and 59) and the backing of many local businesses (see opposite).

We are also grateful to the trust put in us by the many people who paid up front for their copy of the book – numbering more than 200, including advance subscribers (see Pages 114/115).

Hopefully, the book offers a flavour of this wonderful competition and is as comprehensive as records and space allow. At various times throughout its history, coverage of the Mont was sketchy, at best, but every era is covered in some way.

Apologies for any omissions or errors but all information was correct to the best of our knowledge in November 2022. Personal memories do get confused over time and there were some instances of 'first-hand' accounts differing or contradicting versions of events from contemporary sources.

Any corrections will appear on the Mont website – *www.montagucup.com*

The research for this book was done by Chris Brook, who played in the earlier rounds of the competition. He said: "I never got past the semi-final (which, I have no memory of – so I guess must have been away for that game!). My brother also played in the 1991 final.

"My own interest in the Montagu Cup stems from my involvement in a school football competition in the same geographical area – the 99-year-old Totty Cup. As part of the research towards the centenary of that, I was already collecting photographs when I heard something that ignited my passion for the Montagu Cup.

Former England Schoolboys footballer, Jimmy Kelly (Denaby) mentioned that there was once a player who had won the Totty Cup, the Montagu Cup and the FA Cup – George Robledo. I read that George had played in two FA Cup finals for Newcastle United, scoring the winner in 1952. Research confirmed that George had won the Totty Cup twice for Brampton Ellis, scoring 10 goals in two finals.

"For years I was unsure about George's Montagu Cup final appearance. Then, in the 2019 programme, there was a '75 years ago' section that detailed George Robledo scoring in the 1944 Montagu Cup final. It was from this moment that I felt driven to record the rich history of the Mexborough Montagu Hospital Charity Cup."

Those records have been converted into a literary account of the competition by long-standing football author Steven Penny, who admitted: "Two years ago I'd never even heard of the Mont, let alone been aware of its incredible history.

"My first involvement was really by accident. I was writing *Towering Tales and a Ripping Yarn*, a book about the grassroots heroes of Yorkshire football, and heard about the Mont so came along to watch and write a chapter about it.

"I got chatting to Chris and before I knew it I had been persuaded to help produce a book about its remarkable 125 years.

"Barely 18 months on and, despite a move to Suffolk, here it is. Incredibly, I have since discovered that the Robledo brothers' mother is buried in a churchyard barely 100 yards from the front door of my Lowestoft home!

"I hope you enjoy reading this book and reminiscing about your own Mont memories, as much as I have enjoyed working with Chris to put it together."

Family album

Tales of relative Mont success

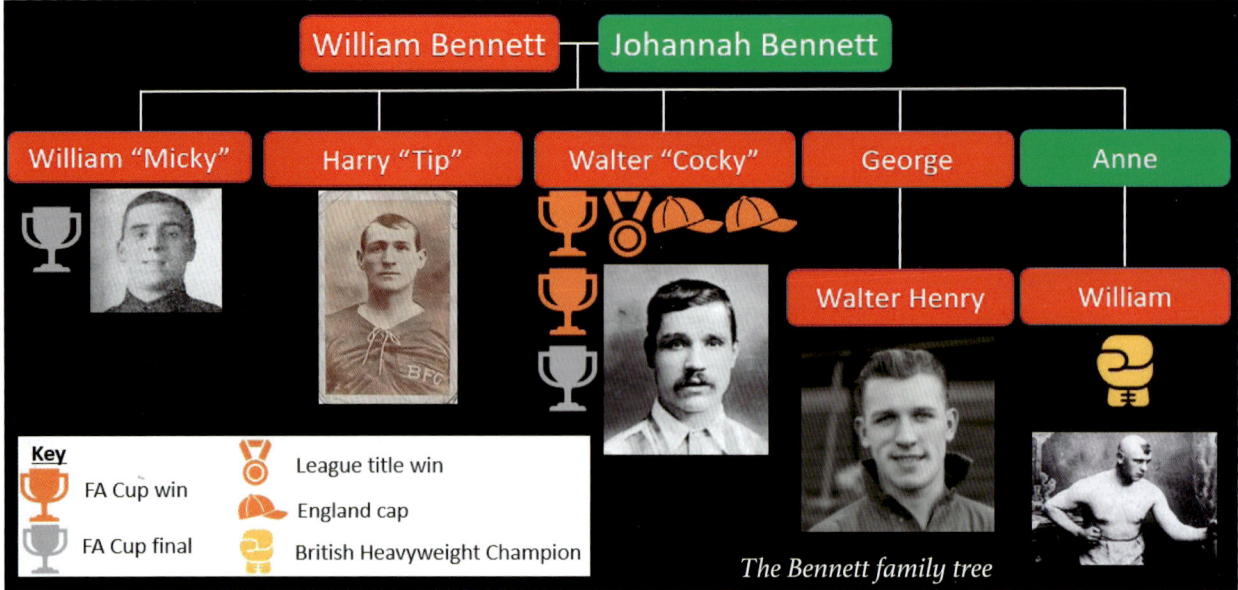

The Bennett family tree

Bennett

The Bennett family came from Mexborough. Barnsley FC historian David Wood went to visit Walter Henry Bennett before he passed away in 2009.

Walter was always aware that his family was special in sporting circles, but it was not until he decided to sign for Barnsley that his father (George) casually mentioned: "I used to play for them."

Up until that time he had no idea that his father had been a professional footballer.

Walter himself played alongside George Robledo in the Barnsley team just after World War Two, scoring 23 times in 38 appearances.

The story was that a generation further back, Walter's grandfather, William, played with all four of his sons – George, William (Micky), Harry (Tip) and Walter (Cocky) in the same Mexborough team that knocked Barnsley out of the FA Cup in 1897/8. However, a later discovery seems to point to it actually being their cousin, also William, who was in the team.

Mexborough had beaten Leeds and Kilnhurst, going on to see off Doncaster Rovers after two replays before losing to Football League side Gainsborough Trinity by a single goal in the final qualifying round.

Walter's grandmother Johannah Bennett (née Brooks), known locally as 'The Institution' and famed for her 'shrieking' during games, also featured in footballing history. After one game at Mexborough in 1894 she made her way on to the field and attacked Barnsley left winger Harry Partridge with her brolly! Sheffield FA excluded Mrs Bennett from the ground for the future – possibly the first football hooligan to receive a ground banning order.

George Bennett played for Barnsley 11 times but was injured in a match against Woolwich Arsenal that ended his fledgling career and he returned to normal life a broken man with no means of an income.

Walter's uncle 'Micky' scored Sheffield Wednesday's goal in their 6-1 1890 FA Cup final defeat against Blackburn Rovers.

Uncle 'Cocky' had 10 seasons in the top flight with Sheffield United after joining them from Mexborough, where he reputedly scored 80 goals in one season from the right wing.

> 'Sheffield FA excluded Mrs Bennett from the ground – possibly the first football hooligan to receive a ground banning order'

He won the Football League title at Bramall Lane and played in three FA Cup finals (two wins and a loss, scoring in the 1899 victory over Derby County and the 1901 defeat by Tottenham), gaining two England caps. They came in the British Home International Championships in 1901 – a 6-0 win against Wales in Newcastle, and a 2-2 draw with Scotland at the original Crystal Palace ground.

He moved to Bristol City and his last match was at Sheffield Wednesday in October 1906. Tragically, just 18 months later, he died in a rockfall at Denaby Main Colliery aged just 34.

Walter Henry's other uncle, 'Tip', lifted the Montagu Cup for Mexborough in 1899. Afterwards, he played 124 times for Barnsley. In 1905 he sent a message to the club to say he was not fit to play against Lincoln. Five days later he had succumbed to pneumonia and passed away at his home at the age of 34. The whole of South Yorkshire football was in mourning and 4,000 people witnessed his interment at Mexborough cemetery.

The sporting connections did not end there though. The three brothers had a sister, Anne, who married John Hague. They named their son William after Anne's father, and William junior became known as William 'Iron' Hague and was British heavyweight boxing champion from 1909 to 1911.

Start of a dynasty. Abe Burkinshaw in the Barnsley team (about 1909). He is the second player from the left in the middle row. He had been a Montagu Cup winner with Kilnhurst in 1907.

Burkinshaw

Three of Kilnhurst's Burkinshaw brothers played professional football at the same time – Jack, Laurie and Ralph. Six descendants of those brothers won Montagu Cup medals, before Nigel won it three times, spanning three decades.

Jack and Laurie played for The Wednesday together and were also at Rotherham Town. They both scored for Wednesday in a 3-0 win over Chelsea on Boxing Day 1913. This is the only time that brothers have scored for the club in the same game.

In another family link, their uncle 'Abe', Abraham, born 1884, played for Barnsley in 1909 and also Rotherham Town, having captained Kilnhurst Town to 1907 Montagu Cup success, in which Jack also played.

As well as Wednesday, Laurie (born 1893), played for Birmingham and Halifax Town. Jack's other teams were Bradford (Park Avenue), Accrington Stanley and Grimsby Town. He was with Kilnhurst WMC during their Mont-winning 1923 season.

The third brother, Ralph (born 1898) played for Bradford City, Bury and Wrexham and also guested for Sheffield United during World War One.

Jack, who was christened John Dean Lewis (born 1890), played for Swindon Town, who were at the time in the Southern League. Despite their non-League status, he was in the team that reached two FA Cup semi-finals (1910 and 1912), the Charity Shield (1911) and the invitational Dubonnet Cup (1910).

Another of the sibling's uncles, Ted, won the 1903 Montagu Cup with Highthorn (Kilnhurst).

Brothers Jack, Laurie and Ralph Burkinshaw

The three brothers also had a cousin, Jas Burkinshaw, who won the Mont in 1914 with Kilnhurst Town.

Moving on a generation, Laurie's son, Jack (born 1911), was in the 1939 Mont-winning Yorkshire Tar Distillers, while Ralph's son, Stan, won the Mont in 1942 with Manvers Main and again in 1946 with Kilnhurst.

In more recent years, Jack's grandson Nigel won the Montagu Cup three times over three decades with Swinton Athletic (1989 – 50 years after his grandad's success), Mexborough Main Street (1999 and 2000).

Nigel with one of his medals

Billups

Andy Billups resurrected Swinton Athletic in 2008 after the club had folded in 2005.

He has featured in four Montagu Cup finals as a manager and one as a player. He won it as a player in 2000 with Mexborough Main Street before chalking up managerial successes in 2020 and 2021 with Swinton, after defeats in the 2014 and 2015 finals.

His younger brother Jon has played in a record seven finals – three wins and four defeats. He was on the winning team in 2011 with Swinton WMC but lost in the following two seasons. He made it four defeats in a row in 2014 and 2015 in the colours of Athletic before a pair of wins for the same team in 2020 and 2021.

The Billups brothers, Jon, top, and Andy

Frith

Father and son Tommy and George Frith have a remarkably similar Montagu Cup record in finals.

Tommy played in the 1923 and 1924 finals for Kilnhurst WMC, scoring in both.

George played in the 1949 and 1950 finals for Kilnhurst Colliery, scoring in both.

George was a superb penalty taker – once scoring 16 in a single season. He played for Thorne Colliery in the Yorkshire League and was paid £3 a match, the same as he got for Newark side Ransome & Marles in the Midland League, which was more than what he was earning at the pit.

George Frith, top, and his father Tommy were both Mont winners

Dawson

A three-generation dynasty of Dawsons enjoyed Montagu Cup final appearances. Sidney scored a record four goals in the Montagu Cup final of 1914 with Kilnhurst Town and went on to play for Grimsby Town.

His son, Eric, played in the 1951 final for Bowbroom WMC, while Sidney's grandson Colin not only won the Montagu Cup three times (1968, 1972 and 1973) but also scored at Wembley (see Pages 96/97).

Two years after winning the Mont, Colin was playing in Matlock Town's finest hour, winning the 1975 FA Trophy final 4-0 against Scarborough.

Colin's wife, Sheila née Frith, also has a connection with the Montagu Cup. Her father, George Frith, won it in 1949 and her grandfather, Tommy Frith won it in 1923. Both played for Kilnhurst teams.

Record scorer Sid Dawson

Eric Dawson in 1951 and, right, more recent times

Colin Dawson with the FA Trophy and, right, more recent times with some of his Montagu Cup awards

Kilnhurst's Pete Scott nods down for Colin Dawson (No.6) to score for Matlock at Wembley in 1975

Kerry

The Kerry family of Kilnhurst had three successive generations of Montagu Cup finalists.

John Arthur Kerry played for Swinton Church in the 1920 Montagu Cup final (although the newspaper report had him down as Currie!).

John Joseph 'Jack' Kerry played in three finals in 1949, 1950 and 1953. The first two for Kilnhurst and the other for Parkgate Welfare. Paul Kerry won the cup in 1968 and 1972 with Swinton Athletic.

Generation game: John, Jack and Paul Kerry have 1920s, 40, 50s, 60s and 70s Montagu Cups to their family name

Needham

Father and son Shaun and Tommy Needham have been involved in a dozen finals, including an amazing one together.

In 2015, Shaun was manager of Memories FC when Tommy scored their winning goal in the 120th minute of a 4-3 comeback.

Shaun has had an involvement in nine finals.

In 1987 he was kit man/physio for Main Street in their 4-2 win. He was then on the committee and assistant manager with the club for their 1995, 1998 and 2007 defeats, as well as their 1999-2001 treble-winning run and further successes in 2005 and 2008. Shaun was then manager of Memories, leading them to a nerve-shattering 4-3 success in 2015.

Son Tommy, meanwhile, featured in that 2015 win and was also on the victorious side for Swinton Athletic in 2020, before coming away with a runners-up medal for Dog Daisy United in 2022.

Tommy is also through to the 2023 final, again with the Dog Daisy team.

A montage of Mont memories for father and son Shaun and Tommy Needham

Shaun Needham on the pitch to celebrate Tommy's late winner in 2015. Shaun and Tommy, right

Oxer

Dean Oxer played in six Montagu Cup finals and won all six of them, scoring three goals in the process.

His son, Brett, is manager of Dog Daisy United, the 2022 beaten finalists, and has also led his team to the 2023 final.

Dean's first final came in 1985 when he scored in a 3-0 win over New Stubbin Colliery for Northgate WMC. Four years later he turned out for Swinton Athletic, helping them to a 2-1 win over Wath Saracens.

Dean was then part of the treble-winning Denaby & Cadeby Miners Welfare side of 1995-97, scoring in the first final – a 2-0 victory over Mexborough Main Street – and playing in part in the following successes against Wath Saracens (4-2 and 2-1).

He completed his six-hit in the colours of Mexborough Main Street in 2000, grabbing the only goal of the game to see off Denaby United.

Team mascot in the 1995 final was Dean's son Brett who, 27 years later, managed Dog Daisy United to the Montagu Cup final. They went down 4-3 in extra-time but he has led them back to the 2023 final.

Progress to the 2023 final came courtesy of qualifying victories over Denaby Main on penalties after a 2-2 draw, Houghton Main 7-0 and Brinsworth DC 5-1. They will meet Central Midlands League side Dearne & District in the final, after the Goldthorpe-based club saw off the challenges of Groves Social 3-0, AFP 2-0 and holders Scawthorpe Athletic 1-0.

Dean Oxer with his son Brett, front, after the 1995 final

Dean Oxer, back row, fourth from right, with the victorious Northgate WMC team in 1987 and, right, Brett Oxer with his Dog Daisy United team at the 2022 Montagu Cup final. His side returns in 2023 looking for a first win.

■ Jake Ford wheels away after scoring for Dog Daisy United in the 2022 final. You can pick out manager Brett Oxer's dad Dean celebrating – arms aloft above and to the left of the Hardware Station advertising board.

The grey-haired man in front of him is Tommy Joyce MBE. He was honoured for all the fund raising he has done through running marathons.

In his youth, 'Mr Mexborough' was a boxing champion and Commonwealth Games bronze medallist for Scotland.

Simon

Terry Simon's Montagu Cup finals have come in clusters, while his son Jake has featured in a record seven finals as a player since coming on as a 16-year old substitute in 2009.

Terry played in three on the bounce as a player (Wath Saracens – 1996, lost 2-4; 1997, lost 0-3; Wombwell Main, won 3-2) before doing the same as a manager more than a decade later (Wombwell Main – 2009, won 4-0; 2010, lost 0-2. Houghton Main – 2011, lost 1-2).

More recently, he featured in four consecutive finals (Houghton Main – 2016, lost 1-3; 2017, won 1-0. Wombwell Main – 2018, lost 0-4; 2019, lost 0-6).

Jake Simon came off the bench to start his Mont collection

Wombwell Main captain Terry Simon with manager Bill Roby after winning the cup in 1998

Jake had a winning start when he came off the bench to help Wombwell Main to a 4-0 victory over Westville in 2009 but was on the losing side in 2010 (for Wombwell) and 2011 (for Houghton Main). He lost again for Houghton in 2016 but got a winners' medal in 2017 before switching back to Wombwell colours for defeats in 2018 and 2019.

One of Terry Simon's Mont treble – 2017 with Houghton Main

Those Watson wonders…

The football career of Billy Watson started in the Dearne Valley in 1911 with Bolton United.

Billy was in the Huddersfield Town team that won the FA Cup in 1922 and went on to win Football League titles in 1924, 1925 and 1926.

Billy's son, Willie was also born in Bolton-on-Dearne and he was a double international, with four caps for England at football and 23 Tests for England at cricket. Willie's most famous innings saved a Test match against Australia at Lord's in 1953 – scoring a dogged 109 runs in almost six hours.

Jack Smelt, far left, lines up for The Wednesday in 1921

Brothers Alf, Len and Tom Smelt all played in the League

Smelt

The four Smelt brothers from Kimberworth, Rotherham, all played League football. Two of them, Alf and Jack played in Kimberworth Old Boys' 1919 Montagu Cup win. Alf was in goal but played both in goal and as a defender for Rotherham County.

Len, born 1883, made his Football League debut with Gainsborough Trinity in 1908 and played for Burnley's famous 'Champions of England' team in 1921. He was still at Turf Moor aged 41, becoming their oldest ever player, and continued playing League football, turning out two years later at Barrow, and later still for non-League Hurst (Manchester) and Frickley Colliery.

Alf, born 1885, played for Chesterfield Town and Mexborough Town before making his Leeds United debut in a 1920 7-0 FA Cup battering of Leeds Steelworks. United had been forced to play two games at the same time, so Smelt was drafted into a makeshift cup XI, while the first team were losing a Division Two match 1-0 at Blackpool. He made only one League appearance for the Peacocks.

Third brother Jack (b. 1895), christened John William, appeared for Mansfield Mechanics, Chesterfield Municipal, Rotherham County and Portsmouth before joining The Wednesday, where he played 16 times, scoring twice in the 1919/20 season. He later turned out for Barrow.

During his wartime service in the 1918/19 season at Rotherham County, he was called upon to play for short-handed opponents Leeds City as a 'guest'.

The final brother, Tom, born 1900, had the most impressive list of clubs, numbering Mexborough Town, Chesterfield Municipal, Rotherham Town, Burnley, Wombwell, Accrington Stanley, Exeter City, Chesterfield, Morecambe, Manchester City, Oldham Athletic, Crewe Alexandra, Scunthorpe & Lindsey United and Rotherham United among his stops during a near-100 game Football League career.

Smith

The three Smith brothers from Conisbrough – Ian, Gary and Trevor – have played in 10 Montagu Cup finals between them.

Ian featured in finals across four decades – the 1980s, 1990s, 2000s and 2010s.

1988: All three played for Denaby & Cadeby Miners Welfare in a win. Ian and Gary scored.

1991: Another win for Denaby & Cadeby and Ian and Gary played, with Gary scoring again.

1996: Ian completed a hat-trick with another win for Denaby & Cadeby but was the only brother involved.

2002, 2003 and 2005: Ian lost with Groves Social before winning at the fourth attempt in 2010.

Ian was also involved with the Conyers team that won the Montagu Cup in 2006 but did not play in the final.

Denaby & Cadeby MW's 1988 Mont-winning Smith brothers

Charlie Taylor, left, his sons Jack, Jimmy and Walt, above, and, right, grandson 'Spud' with Swinton in 1980

Taylor

Charlie Taylor played Midland League football for Mexborough in 1922/23, against the first teams of Doncaster Rovers and Rotherham, and three of his sons won the Montagu Cup, with a grandson making it eight Mont medals between them.

Jimmy Taylor was a Mont winner in 1946 for Kilnhurst and his son Alan 'Spud' added a generation with victory for Swinton Athletic in 1980.

Jack put his name on the honours list in 1949 and 1950, while Walt picked up medals in 1949 and 1950 with Kilnhurst (a shared win and runners-up) and victory in 1961 and 1962 with Parkgate Welfare. He also won two Rotherham Charity Cups.

Another brother, Bill, also played for Kilnhurst but damaged his knee at an early age, while another, Charlie junior, was an RAF bomber pilot.

Watkin

Glyn 'Taffy' Watkin scored in the 1959 Montagu Cup final for winners Tom Hill and in 1968 was in the defeated High Terrace XI.

In 1991 he lifted the Mont again as assistant manager at Denaby & Cadeby Miners Welfare.

Taffy's son, Steve, won the Mont in 1988, also with Denaby & Cadeby MW.

Taffy' Watkin with his 1959 trophy in more recent years

Whitehouse

Jack Whitehouse was the secretary of High Terrace when they played Swinton Athletic in the 1968 Montagu Cup final.

He was one of seven of the Whitehouse family involved that day and overall Jack's descendants have gained 17 Montagu Cup medals between them.

Patriarch Jack, left, and his sons Keith, Colin, 'Shona' and Ken

Jack's footballing descendants:
- First generation:
Sons – Colin snr, Keith, Ken and John 'Shona'.
- Second generation:
Grandsons – Colin snr's sons: Malc, Colin jnr and Glyn.
Ken's sons: Paul and Dean.
John's son: Ryan.
Keith's son: Michael.
- 3rd generation:
Great-grandsons – Michael's son: Billy.
Malc's son: Tim.

Grandsons Malc (at the 1972 Mont final), Colin junior and Glyn

The Magnificent 1968 Whitehouse Seven...

1 Jack – High Terrace secretary; 2 Ken – High Terrace centre back; 3 Keith – High Terrace midfield player; 4 John 'Shona' – Swinton left-half; 5 Colin junior – Swinton winger; 6 Malc – Swinton striker; 7 Colin senior – Swinton trainer.

Grandsons Paul, Dean, Ryan and Michael

Mont medallists:

1951 – Colin snr: Runner-up with Bowbroom WMC.
1966 – Ken and Keith: Winners with High Terrace.
1967 – John and Ken: Winners with High Terrace.
1968 – Shona, Colin jnr and Malc: Winners with Swinton Athletic.
1968 – Ken and Keith: Runners-up with High Terrace.
1972 – Malc: Winner with Swinton Athletic.
1980 – Glyn: Winner with Swinton Athletic.
1985 – Paul: Winner with Northgate.
1996 – Ryan: Runner-up with Wath Saracens.
1997 – Ryan: Runner-up with Wath Saracens.
1998 – Tim: Runner-up with Mexborough Main Street.
1999 – Tim: Winner with Mexborough Main Street.
2000 – Tim: Winner with Mexborough Main Street.
2011 – Tim: Winner with Swinton WMC.

And at an elite level...

1983 – Dean was with Barnsley in the second tier of the Football League from 1981-1984, later playing for Torquay United.
2017 – Billy played for Leeds United in the FA Cup, previously for Doncaster Rovers and is now in the National League North with Chorley,

Great grandsons Tim and Billy

having also played for Guiseley, FC Halifax Town, Alfreton Town, Spennymoor Town and The New Saints (where he played in the Europa League) among others.

Ian (Malc's son) is deserving of a medal for the many hours he has contributed to volunteering in local football.

He is a football coach and referee.

Malc's son Ian is key off the field

Wilkinson

Shaun Wilkinson won his first Montagu Cup at the tender age of 17 and within 11 days of his 20th birthday had three to his name.

That was an impressive start to a dynasty that now sees his twin sons chalking up more Mont records.

Shaun played for Mexborough Main Street in the 1983 final and won it again in 1984 for Main Street and again in 1986, this time in the colours of Swinton Athletic against Main Street. He now works for Stelrad – the cup and this book's main sponsors – and presented the trophy in 2020, when his sons, Alex and Curtis, were in the winning Swinton team.

Both scored in that match and played again in Swinton's 2021 win. Alex made it a hat-trick of final appearances in 2022 but Curtis missed out, having played in an earlier round for Swinton Athletic, who the brothers play for on Saturdays.

This year, they are both in the Sunday League Dog Daisy United squad and are looking forward to the 2023 final.

Shaun Wilkinson with sons Alex, left, and Curtis with the 2022 Mont

Shaun Wilkinson, left, with his winning Swinton Mont teammates Ian Cotton and Gary Hough in 1986

Scan this QR code to watch the Wilkinson twins combine for the goal of the game by Curtis in 2020.

Decades

A year by year summary of the Montagu Cup

1936 winners Wath Road Athletic

Harry 'Tip' Bennett 1899

Sid Dawson scored four goals in the 1914 final – a cup record

The ball hits the net for the 2015 winner

Darfield Bridge celebrate their 1926 victory

Houghton Main's 1975 trophy haul

1897-1909

1897
Ecclesfield 2 Newhill 0

The first Montagu Cup final was played on Easter Monday at Mexborough Club, Hampden Road, and saw a win for Ecclesfield.

It proved to be a violent encounter as the following newspaper report reflected:

> "Newhill, on Monday, were defeated in the final of the Montagu Charity Cup by two goals to nil. The game was anything but a pleasant one, and with a less competent official than George Parkin behind the whistle would probably have ended in a free fight. As it was he had all his work cut out to restrain the ebullition of temper of the performers."

A poem also appeared as a summary of the match but, remarkably, neither version of the report included details of who got the goals.

Later research determined those first scorers were Cutts and Hemingfield.

```
No. 326.—THEY END THEIR DREAM.
    'Tis sweet in happy youth,
        When the world seems fair,
    In dreams to build
        Grand castles in the air,
    But then, alas! alack!
        The fates we deem
    So kind, turn cold and cruel,
        And end our dream.
    With Newhill I am bound
        To sympathise,
    Ambition lured them
        With a promised prize.
    In Ecclesfield they met
        A stronger team,
    They lost the pot, and there
        They end their dream.
                G. R. TENNYSON-SIMS.
The final tie for the Mexborough Montagu Charity
Cup tie, between Ecclesfield and Newhill, was brought
off on the Mexborough ground on Monday morning,
before a splendid attendance, and in beautiful weather.
Half-time arrived with Ecclesfield holding a substan-
tial lead of two goals.
    At the finish Newhill had to retire defeated by two
goals to nil.
                            ROVER.
```

1898
Kilnhurst v Birdwell (* = replayed)

The second final turned out to be the match that never was.

Birdwell beat Kilnhurst 2-1 in the first match but a replay was ordered after the defeated side put in a complaint about the eligibility of two players, Hall and Wilkinson, and the cup and trophies had to be returned.

William 'Dutch' Gladwin had scored Kilnhurst's goal in front of a crowd of 2,000. The replay took place two weeks later in front of a crowd of 1,000 and it was again marred by problems with Kilnhurst players walking off after a decision went against them and an objection resulted in the linesman being replaced by a "spectator".

Two Gladwins played in both matches for Kilnhurst. As well as Dutch, Peter Gladwin is also mentioned. Kilnhurst won the restaging 1-0. Only one Gladwin brother played, and scored the 'winner', but it is not clear which sibling it was.

Not that it matters because another complaint was received, this time from Birdwell, who objected to the inclusion of Caterer in their opponents' line-up. Once more the complaint was sustained and a replay ordered but it would appear that was never played and the final was eventually declared void.

Dutch Gladwin lost his life at Gallipoli in December 1915 (see Page 109). He had signed for Doncaster Rovers after the 1898 Mont.

Another player earning instant elevation after his Mont exploits was Francis Pepper, who signed for Sheffield United the day after the replay. He made no appearances at Bramall Lane but a few months later joined Newton Heath and played seven times for the future Manchester United.

He died in Rotherham aged 38 in 1914.

William Gladwin

1899
Mexborough Town 3 Wath 1

Harry "Tip" Bennett was the captain in 1899 and played alongside his brother George. Their family has an amazing story – told in more detail on Page 12.

It was Mexborough Town's reserves that played in the final as the first team had a fixture clash.

Four days after the final there was a benefit match for Tip at Mexborough, in which at least two England internationals played – Bill 'Fatty' Foulke and Harry Ruddlesdin.

The benefit match is believed to be because he was leaving to play for Barnsley after 12 seasons at Mexborough. He played for Barnsley for the next six seasons before dying of pneumonia aged 34 just a few days after playing for Barnsley reserves in 1905.

Mexborough's Harry 'Tip' Bennett

1900

Why wasn't there a Mont held in 1900? Because the cup committee never got round to organising it!

A reporter for the local paper included a few 'reminders' and suggested that around October they should give the job to someone else, but neglected to pass the information on properly, by which time it was too late anyway. In a later edition – the committee replied and blamed the clubs.

1901 Montagu Cup final players, from left: Alf Streets, Billy Linward and Walter Langton

Doncaster's first team soon after the Montagu Cup final (in which the reserves had to play).

1901
Doncaster Rovers 5 Mexborough Thursday 2

Unlike 1912-13, when Rovers entered a reserve XI, they treated this as a first-team competition.

However, the final clashed with a Midland League game at home to Hinckley Town (which Rovers won 5-0). Therefore Rovers sent their second XI to Mexborough on April 6 for the Montagu Cup final and still managed to win.

This was one of Walter Langton's 18 seasons for the Rovers.

Billy Linward got their fifth goal and next season was a regular with West Ham. After that he moved to Woolwich Arsenal.

Alf Streets was in the Mexborough Thursday team. In 1907, aged 30 he was confined to a bath-chair due to a serious illness. A benefit match was played for him with some real star players.

1902
Denaby United 3 Newhill 0

Another four-figure crowd watched Denaby chalk up their first success, courtesy of goals from Hardy, Chadfield and McNeil.

In the 1900s, victorious teams walked back to their clubs from Mexborough, accompanied by a brass band playing Handel's 'See the conqu'ring hero comes'.

Denaby were met by a wildly cheering crowd at the railway crossing and proceeded to the Denaby Main Hotel and their clubhouse, at the Reresby Arms.

1903
Highthorn Mission 2 Wath Athletic 1 *

1903 finalists Tommy Thorpe and Tommy Tompkins

Highthorn was a standalone football club, although the hamlet of Highthorn, with no more than three-dozen houses is within the boundaries of Kilnhurst.

A crowd of 4,000 was in attendance on Easter Saturday for a replay after the teams had drawn 1-1 two weeks earlier.

Just days after the final Tommy Tompkins and Charlie Bisby were signed by Doncaster Rovers.

Tommy Thorpe (Highthorn) went on to play in goal for Barnsley and holds the record for being their oldest player (40) and their only goalkeeper to score a goal.

He also played first-class cricket for Northamptonshire.

His wife, Sarah and eldest daughter, Olive, died within two weeks of one another in 1918 during the Spanish Flu pneumonia pandemic.

Both are buried in Kilnhurst. Matt Ardron and Len Ardron played for Highthorn. Len's son was Wally Ardron.

Billy Biggs, Charlie Tayles, R McNeil and Rodgers, pictured in 1907, played for Mexborough Town in the 1904 and 1905 finals

Wombwell Main 1906 – the first recorded photo of the Montagu Cup

1904
Mexborough Town 4 Rotherham Town 1

Billy Westwood (inset) played for Mexborough Town in this final. He went on to play for Bristol Rovers but died near Arras in 1917, during the First World War.

Billy's grandson Dennis 'The Menace' Priestley was darts world champion in 1991 and 1994.

There was ill feeling after this final. So much so, that when they met again shortly afterwards there was a riot.

Speight for Rotherham was seriously injured and they had to send for a cab to convey him home.

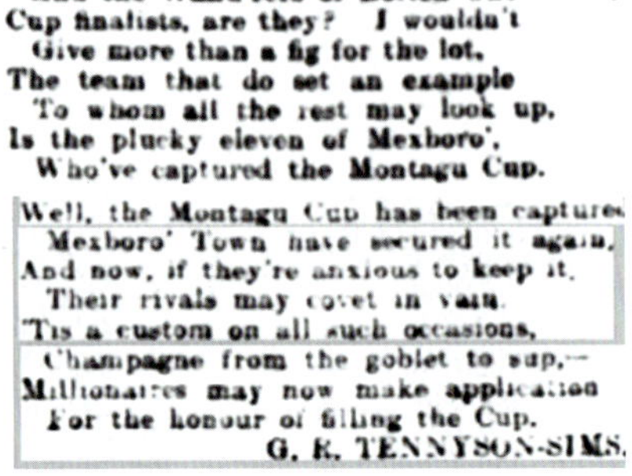

Mexborough players and officials were attempting to board their waggonette and a number of spectators swarmed round and threw large stones and bricks, with three players receiving nasty injuries – Powell, a broken thumb; Rogers, a heavily bruised thigh; and Briggs, a severe blow to the knee. Some eight or 10 policemen prevented further mischief.

1905 finalist Tommy Hakin went on to play for Grimsby Town

1905
Mexborough Town 1 South Kirkby 0

A second consecutive win for Mexborough Town but both finals were played away from Hampden Road – at Denaby in 1904 and Bolton-upon-Dearne in 1905 – to avoid any claims of 'home' advantage.

1906
Wombwell Main 2 South Kirkby 1

Wombwell Main won the Montagu Cup, the Rotherham Charity Cup and Barnsley Beckett Hospital Cup – a feat never done before or since.

You can make out the three Holmes brothers on the team photograph. Ezra Holmes signed for Football League side Gainsborough Trinity, scoring 12 goals in 41 appearances as centre forward, despite his short stature. He went on to sign for Birmingham City for a huge £400 fee but only played twice.

A poem to celebrate the 1904 final

No. 592.—A BALLAD OF THE MONTAGU CUP.

Go talk of your Manchester City,
And the Wand'rers of Bolton who 'Trot,'
Cup finalists, are they? I wouldn't
Give more than a fig for the lot.
The team that do set an example
To whom all the rest may look up,
Is the plucky eleven of Mexboro'.
Who've captured the Montagu Cup.

Well, the Montagu Cup has been captured
Mexboro' Town have secured it again,
And now, if they're anxious to keep it.
Their rivals may covet in vain.
'Tis a custom on all such occasions,
Champagne from the goblet to sup,—
Millionaires may now make application
For the honour of filling the Cup.
G. R. TENNYSON-SIMS.

1907
Kilnhurst Town 2 Parkgate & Rawmarsh 0

Willis Rippon and Jack Burkinshaw scored for Kilnhurst.

The latter went on to a long Football League career with Grimsby, The Wednesday, Bradford (Park Avenue) and Accrington Stanley before becoming an early overseas export when he went to Chicago Bricklayers.

Rippon too played for Grimsby, as well as Bristol City, Arsenal, Brentford and also outside England, although in his case it was Hamilton Academical.

Willis Rippon was on target for Kilnhurst

1908
Hickleton Main 3 Parkgate & Rawmarsh 1 *

The third Mont final to go to a replay proved to be a goal feast. The teams shared six goals in the initial staging in front of 1,500 fans before Hickleton emerged victorious just four days later with a midweek crowd reduced by a third.

1909
Goldthorpe Institute 3 Parkgate & Rawmarsh 1 *

Another replay brought Rawmarsh & Parkgate's third successive final defeat… but at least they won the Rotherham Charity Cup.

The first staging at Wath saw a 1-1 draw with a crowd of 1,500, an attendance repeated six days later at Hampden Road.

The Mexborough Montagu Hospital Charity Cup

The actual cup was made and assayed at London Assay office in 1896 by a silverware firm called Charles Stuart Harris.

Harris was a silversmith between 1852 and 1897, running the business that became C.S. Harris & Sons Ltd in 1897. Originally making spoons and forks, the firm was based in Hatton Garden and Clerkenwell, London, from 1892.

The company traded until 1934 when it was taken over by Israel Freeman & Sons. Freeman moved to London in the 1920s from Sheffield.

The detail on the trophy is all hand-chased and would have taken a considerable amount of time when it was made in 1896.

It weighs 147 Troy ozs (4.6kg) and in 1897 was worth £85 – that's about £8,000 today. Reports in 1913 and 1915 said that the Montagu Cup was the most valuable in England and had a higher silver content than the FA Cup.

However, unlike the FA Cup, the Montagu Cup is the original trophy that was first presented in 1897.

After fire damage at Mexborough Main Street Club the trophy was refurbished by Bob Lamb, a Mexborough-based silversmith who has a lifetime of experience of producing and repairing trophies for many organisations.

The fire left the Montagu Cup totally black with a hole in one of the flutes (the curves looping around the cup).

The cup is made of sterling silver and Bob said: "It is 925 silver. That means that 925 out of 1,000 parts are silver. If it was 1,000 out of 1,000 it would be too soft, so other metals are added to make it more workable – but only 7.5 per cent."

One of Bob's commissions was in the early 1990s when he made two replica Calcutta Cups after the rugby players damaged the original.

Supporters of Askern Road Working Men's Club assure us that the Mont holds 17 and a half pints of liquid – they did not specify whether that was beer or spirits!

Denaby United's victorious 1915 squad and club officials. It was the last final before a break for World War One

1910-1919

1910
Hickleton Main 2
Mexborough Reserves 0

Two goals from McKenning secured the Mont for Hickleton after they progressed from an energy-sapping semi-final.

Conisbrough Swifts had won the semi-final at the fourth attempt, after three drawn matches but Hickleton appealed that they had played an ineligible player.

They won their appeal after initially being refused by the cup committee. It was passed to the Sheffield & Hallamshire FA, who ordered a rematch.

That went 1-0 in favour of Hickleton, only for Swifts to object, necessitating a sixth match, which went 3-0 in Hickleton's favour.

The teams had also drawn twice in the league during the season.

Hickleton were obviously confident of victory in the final because they took their own band and marched back home with the band playing 'See the conqu'ring hero comes'.

Goalkeeper Willis Walker won the Mont in 1913 with Doncaster Rovers and went on to complete more than 300 Football League appearances for Leeds City, South Shields, Bradford (Park Avenue) and Stockport County, as well as scoring more than 1,000 first-class runs a season 10 times for Nottinghamshire CCC (picture: trentbridge.co.uk). He served in the Royal Navy during World War One and died aged 99 in 1991

1911
Hickleton Main 3 Ryecroft Wesleyans 1 *

Wesleyans were a Sunday School League side and near the bottom of the table but came close to an upset. A crowd of 2,000 saw T Sutton score their goal in a 1-1 draw with Hickleton, for whom Russell was on target. Two goals from Jack Eades and one from Leonard gave Hickleton victory in the replay. Russell scored for Wesleyans, who also lost in the final of the Rotherham Charity Cup.

1912
Hickleton Main 2
Frickley Colliery 0

Among the Hickleton team this season was Joe Smith, who went on to play for Birmingham and Chesterfield. He served in the 17th Battalion, Middlesex Regiment – the so-called Footballers' Battalion – in northern France.

He rose to the rank of Company Sergeant Major and was killed on November 13, 1916, near the end of the Battle of the Somme (see Page 109).

Joe was mentioned in despatches for displaying considerable bravery after "being wounded, again dashed into battle, only to be shot down" and is commemorated at Serre Road Cemetery No.1.

The final was played at Wath but there is no record of the scorers as Hickleton became the first club to claim a Mont hat-trick.

Hickleton Main's 1912 Montagu Cup winner Joe Smith was killed in action

1913
Doncaster Rovers Reserves 2 Hickleton Main 0

A fourth consecutive final appearance for Hickleton ended in defeat. They had been given an extra chance after the first match was abandoned due to bad weather, with Rovers leading 3-0 at the time. However, they failed to take the second chance and Tommy Astill, Shackleton and Jack Nuttall were on target for Rovers' second string.

1914
Kilnhurst Town 6 Sth Yorkshire Hotel 1

Sid Dawson scored four goals, a record that has never been beaten, to go with a brace from J Clarke. It was equalled in 2019 by Joker's Ross Duggan.

Charlie Bentham and Ernie Hobson played in previous rounds as they both got medals. Charlie was killed in World War One. Badly injured on the first day of the Somme, July 1916, he survived the battlefield only to die three weeks later in Wrexham hospital, aged 26. He is buried just inside the gate in St Thomas Churchyard, Kilnhurst (see Page 109).

Sergeant-Major J. Smith.

We regret to report that Sergeant-Major J. Smith, of Swinton and Thurnscoe, was killed on Nov. 13, 1916. The news was contained in a letter from his Orderly-Corporal W. Wilson, who also comes from Thurnscoe. Sergeant Smith was a prominent football player, well-known in South Yorkshire. His home was at Swinton. He joined the Hickleton Main team, afterwards being transferred to Birmingham. He then joined Chesterfield Town, with which club he was when he joined the Footballers' Battalion (Middlesex Regiment). He quickly won promotion. He enlisted in January, 1915. He was made sergeant in England, and was promoted to Company-Sergeant-Major in France. He came over on leave last Easter, when he married Miss Florrie Fawcett, daughter of Mrs. Fawcett and the late Mr. D. Fawcett, of Thurnscoe. Particulars will be printed in our next issue.

1915
Denaby United 2
Mexborough Grand Central Loco 0 *

The final match before a break caused by World War One saw Denaby mark the departure of six players who had enlisted, with a second replay win.

Glennon and Atkins were on target for the Mexborough side in a 2-2 draw. No result is available for the first replay but Owen Bransby and Jepson repeated their goals from the first encounter in the decider to secure a three-year hold on the Mont.

1916 and 1917

No finals were played for two seasons due to World War One.

1918 *
Mexborough Rovers 2 Denaby Mission 0

The decision was made to revive the competition in March 1918 with four clubs invited to compete. The final went to three replays with Mexborough Rovers eventually beating Denaby Mission.

It had taken two matches to decide the finalists but four more to produce an eventual winner with goals from Hackford and Percy Beaumont securing the silverware!

Admission to the final cost 4d, with a place in the stand 1d extra.

A ladies competition was also run with Denaby Munitions Girls meeting Barnsley NPF in the final.

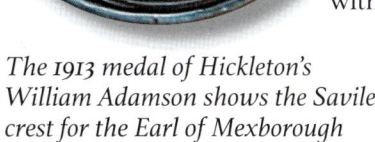

The 1913 medal of Hickleton's William Adamson shows the Savile crest for the Earl of Mexborough

Kilnhurst with the 1914 Montagu Cup, including record scorer Sid Dawson, right

William Adamson's 1913 medal, left pair, one from 1915 (thanks to Pamela Purdy) and the 1919 version, right pair, which was presented to Jack Barker (courtesy of Elaine Maden and Maxine Manion-License)

1919
Kimberworth Old Boys 2
Denaby United 0 *

Percy Beaumont scored in the 1918 final's third replay

Goals from Wightman and George Dobson secured the Mont for Kimberworth. Their team was soon broken up though, with nine of their squad playing in the Football League the following season as far afield as Portsmouth, Norwich and Coventry, as well as Rotherham and Barnsley.

The Old Boys also won the Sheffield Junior Cup, in front of a 6,000 crowd at Bramall Lane.

What a record! The following shows where members of last season's Kimberworth Old Boys' team are now operating:—J. Smelt (Portsmouth), A. Smelt (Mexborough), W. Simmonite, J. Harrison, S. Taylor (Rotherham County), J. Herbert, E. Broadhead (Norwich City), S. Sleight (Silverwood), F. Howe (Coventry), V. Whitham and G. Dobson (Barnsley).

Green 'Un September 6, 1919. Most of these would have played in the Montagu Cup final a few months earlier

Jack Barker played for Denaby United in the final and had scored in the semi-final.

In his twilight years, he gifted his medal to a seven-year-old Swinton neighbour, Mark Licence, in Slade Road. Licence went on to win the Montagu Cup three times himself.

Alf Smelt, George Dobson and James Edward 'Jimmy' Broadhead won the cup in 1919 with Kimberworth Old Boys

Hat-trick heroes

Only seven players have scored hat-tricks in Montagu Cup finals

1914 – 4 goals: Sid Dawson (Kilnhurst Town)
1940 – 3 goals: Cyril Grant (Manvers Main)
1942 – 3 goals: John Cocker (Manvers Main)
1950 – 3 goals: Les Swales (Rawmarsh Welfare)
1964 – 3 goals: Marshall Robshaw (Swinton Ath)
1966 – 3 goals: Peter Davies (High Terrace)
2019 – 4 goals: Ross Duggan (Joker)

Clockwise, from top left: Sid Dawson, Ross Duggan, Les Swales and Cyril Grant

1920-1929

1920
Swinton Discharged Soldiers & Sailors 1
Swinton Church Bible Class 0

A record total of 34 teams entered the first competition of the 1920s and winners Swinton Discharged Soldiers & Sailors were indebted to goalkeeper Jack Palmer.

He saved a penalty in the final, which meant V Temple's goal was enough to secure the Montagu Cup against their town rivals.

Jack went on to become president of the Coal Miners Union and was also a justice of the peace and councillor.

Kilnhurst WMC's 1923 players and committee line up in Dr Aitken's garden at the top of Victoria Street

Jack Palmer saved a penalty in the 1920 final

The Discharged Soldiers & Sailors completed a cup double with victory over Kimberworth Old Boys in the Rotherham Charity Cup. It came after they had lost in front of a 4,000 Millmoor crowd but appealed against their opponents using Rotherham County professional Topham in their line-up. The rematch went 3-1 in the Swinton side's favour.

1921
Parkgate Christ Church 1
Barnburgh Colliery 0

Harry Maycock was the goal hero for Christ Church but Barnburgh bounced back the following year.

1922
Barnburgh Colliery 4
Swinton Discharged Soldiers 3 *

Marshall and Foster traded goals in the Easter Monday final but a week later Barnburgh emerged victorious in the replay.

It was another tight affair, needing extra time to decide matters and with the Swinton side hitting the bar.

1923
Kilnhurst WMC 4
Sandhill Juniors 1 *

Oscar Allen was goalkeeper for Barnburgh in the 1921 and 1922 finals

Kilnhurst marked their victory by lining up for a team picture in the garden of football supporter Dr Aitken, a long-serving and much liked Kilnhurst doctor.

All members of the Sandhill team were under the age of 20.

L Meadows (Kilnhurst goal-keeper): "We didn't enter the cup just to carry off the cup, but in remembrance of the good work that was being done in the house (hospital) over yonder." BL Smith presenting (chairman of the hospital sports committee): "When His Majesty presents the English Cup, he would not have more pleasure in doing so than he had in presenting the beautiful Mont Cup to the successful team. Those in the Mexborough District know that by the competition for the Montagu Hospital Cup they were doing something to help unfortunate people who could not help themselves."

scoring 77 goals. He also appeared for the Football League representative team twice and his one England appearance came in 1934, a 2-1 defeat to Czechoslovakia in Prague.

He finished his career with Swansea Town and non-League Stourbridge.

The 1924 Askern Road WMC winning team, above, and, right, Joe Beresford, who scored in the final and went on to play in the FA Cup final, as well as earning one England cap

> The outstanding player was Beresford, the Askern inside-right, who was easily the best player on the field, and whose work was clever and cunning throughout. Teams:—

1924
Askern Road WMC 3 Kilnhurst WMC 1

Joe Beresford got the third goal for the Doncaster side in this Good Friday clash and ended up playing for England during nine seasons at Aston Villa, as well as in the 1937 FA Cup final for Preston.

His grandson Dean Beresford tells his story:

"Joe grew up in Bentley and worked as a pit-pony stable-lad at the pit in the early 1920s.

"He was playing for Mexborough by 1924 (he then moved on to Mansfield before joining Aston Villa in 1927). He had been spotted by Mexborough officials as the dominating figure in a Montagu Cup final at Hampden Road.

"Joe scored more than 100 goals in two seasons with Mexborough in the Midland League and cup ties."

Joe, who died in 1978 just before his 72nd birthday, played more than 300 Football League games,

1925
Darfield Bridge 3
South Elmsall United Services 2

Supporters got on their bikes for this final with many of the fans cycling to Mexborough from Darfield and South Elmsall.

Mynett, Tyler and Roberts netted for the victors, with Martin and McGuire on target for the Elmsall side.

However, a month after the final, the Mexborough FA suspended the Darfield Bridge secretary and their player, Tyler, as he had been banned at the time of the Montagu Cup final.

There is no record of an appeal or a rematch.

George Fearon's 1925 medal

1926
Darfield Bridge 1 Goldthorpe United 0

Smallwood got the only goal of the game to decide this match.

The 1924 trophy presentation   *1926 Montagu Cup winners Darfield Bridge*

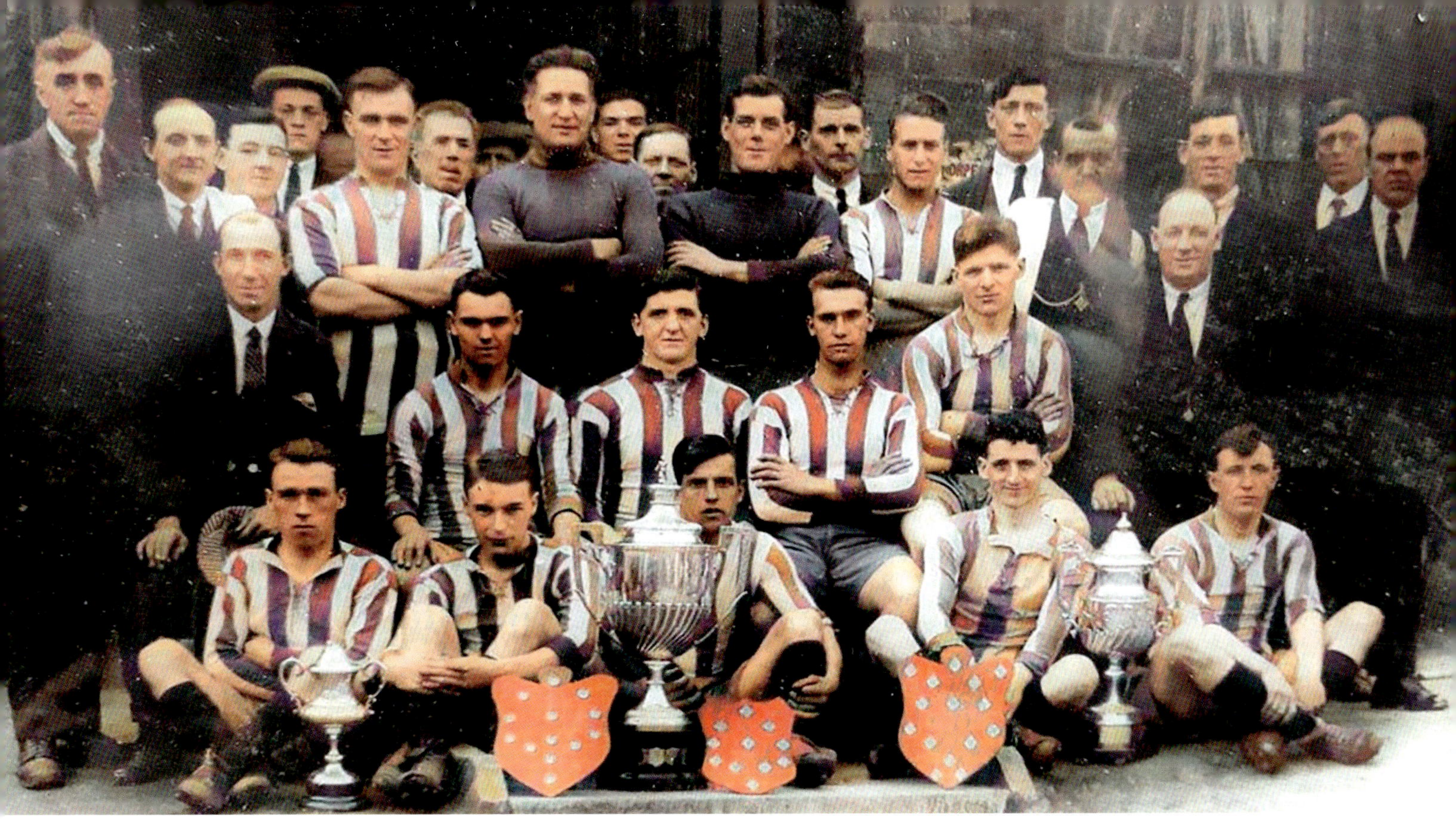

Goldthorpe United with the 1927 Montagu Cup

THEIRS AT LAST.

The Ashwood Road captain received the Montagu Cup at Hampden Road, Mexboro', on Wednesday evening, after his team had beaten Roman Terrace in the replayed final tie, 2—1; but only after an unprecedented wait. An objection was raised by Roman Terrace on the ground that Hughes, of Ashwood Road, was not registered according to the rules of the Football Association; and only after a meeting on the ground, and an urgent messenger had been sent to make inquiries, did the board governing the competition decide that the protest could not be upheld. The presentation of the trophy was thus delayed till 9-30 p.m.—with the result that our photographer had to do his work by flashlight.

The portrait inset is that of Hughes, the player over whom the pother occurred. The matter is fully dealt with in our sports columns.

1927
Goldthorpe United 3
South Yorkshire Chemical Works 0

Goldthorpe bounced back from the previous year's defeat with a comfortable victory courtesy of goals from Jim Hadlington 2 and Goodman.

The final witnessed mass singing by the 3,000 spectators, 'conducted by Mr CH Sanders' accompanied by the Goldthorpe Ambulance Brigade band.

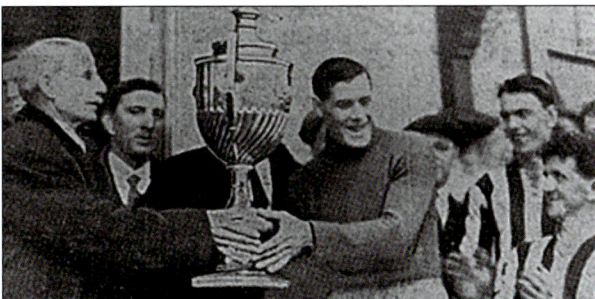

Captain S Hadlington receives the 1927 cup after Goldthorpe beat South Yorkshire Chemical Works

1928
Ashwood Road WMC 2
Roman Terrace Athletic 1 *

Another final was hit by scandal with yet another appeal. The Good Friday encounter had finished goalless but Wrack and Bailey were on the scoresheet 19 days later.

However, Roman Terrace objected to Hughes playing and a messenger was sent to Rotherham, delaying the presentation of the trophy by two hours until 9.30pm.

In the end the result stood but the photographer had to use a flash light and it must be the only presentation where the captain received the trophy wearing a suit!

About 300 fans had waited two hours for the presentation.

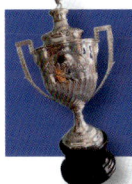

The earliest Montagu Cup match report found is from Swinton Town's 3-0 win against Swinton Trinity on January 18, 1897

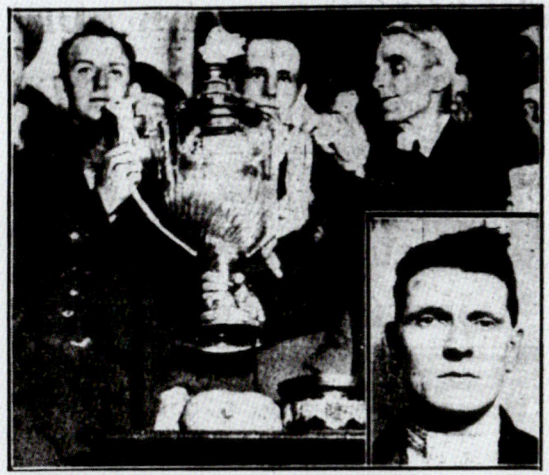

1929
Bolton Albion 2 Conisbrough Welfare 0

A mascot called Bower got to hold the trophy after two goals from George Walker had seen Bolton Albion beat Conisbrough.

THE HARVEST.

GOLDTHORPE United Football Club's team, which has had a brilliant season, and the trophies which it has won. In the centre, the Montagu Cup.

JIM Hadlington re-accepting the Montagu Cup, which Goldthorpe have held for the last twelve months, from Mr. G. H. Cooper, after the final tie with Broomhill at Wath on Friday.

Goldthorpe United enjoyed a prolific period at the start of the 1930s

1930-1939

1930
Goldthorpe United 3
Highgate Halfway House 1 *

The 1930s proved relatively uneventful in Mont history, after the dramas of so many appeals in previous years.

Denman, Frank Chivers and S Chivers scored to enable Goldthorpe to repeat their 1927 success after a 1-1 draw, in which they were grateful for an own goal from Highgate's Skitt.

1931
Goldthorpe United 1
Broomhill 0

The first of a string of finals played on Good Friday and it was business as usual for Goldthorpe, who also reached the third qualifying round of the FA Cup.

Riley got their goal in a final played at Wath in front of 2,000 spectators.

Goldthorpe United, 1931 winners. Picture includes: W Pape, Shepard, Schofield, Hudson, Speight (goalkeeper), Finney, Barker (linesman), Mellor, Raynor, J Hadlington, Critchley and Wise (trainer).

1932
Thorpe Hesley 3 Thurnscoe Vics 1 *

Sid Mace scored three for Vics but was still a loser. He got both goals in a 2-2 draw before grabbing the consolation in the replay at Wath. Hague and an opponent got the Hesley goals in the first match with Sylvester 2 and Ashton netting in the replay.

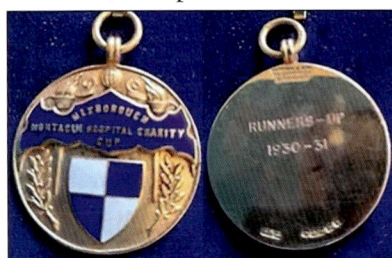

Charlie Ashcroft got a medal for winning the 1931 final, despite not appearing in it. He had, however, played in previous rounds, including the semi-final

1935: Cudworth St Mary's were the first team to score six in a final for 21 years

1933
Thurnscoe Vics 1
Cudworth Village 0
Whitehead was on the mark to see Vics make a swift return to the final, this time with a cup to show for their efforts.

1934
Mexborough Athletic 2
Silverwood Colliery 0
Athletic became the third 'Mexborough' team to lift the cup, following in the footsteps of Town and Rovers, thanks to goals from Roome and Moxon.

1935
Cudworth St Mary's 6
Wath Main 1
A brace apiece from George Blenkinsop and Paddy Poole, plus other goals from Charlie Corns and Sam Turnock saw St Mary's chalk up the first six-goal cup final haul since 1914.

1936
Wath Road Athletic 3 Rawmarsh Welfare 1
Former Manchester City and England star Sam Cowan presented the medals at this final. A ball autographed by the City XI, donated by Mexborough-born City legend Eric Brook, was also presented.

Athletic had been beaten in an earlier round by holders Cudworth St Mary's but they were expelled after being found guilty of fielding an ineligible player.

Wath Road won the 1936 Mont, despite having lost in an earlier round

Northcliffe captain Arthur Roberts at 1937's presentation

Fans watch during a blizzard in 1937

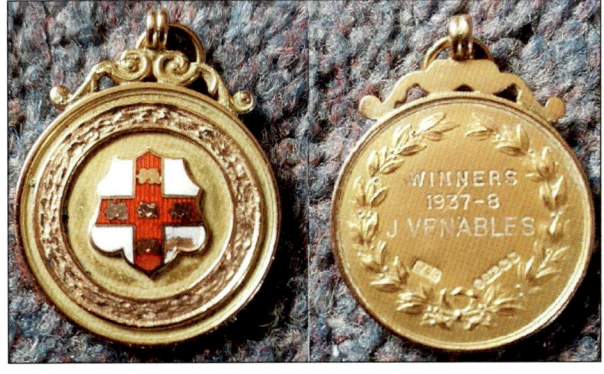
Joe Venables' 1938 winners' medal. Joe is the uncle of book co-author Chris Brook, who was unaware of the link before he started his research

1937
Northcliffe WMC 4
Wombwell Station Lane 1
The Montagu Cup final returned to Mexborough's Hampden Road after a six-year spell at Wath.

1938
Thurnscoe Vics 3 Silverwood Colliery 0
Manchester City and England winger Eric Brook again donated an autographed ball for a final that saw Sid Mace make a third appearance for Vics.

The Mont returned to Hampden Road in 1937 and saw Northcliffe Working Men's Club emerge victorious

1939
Yorkshire Tar Distillers 5 Baker & Bessemer 0

There was a problem with the traditional Good Friday date because *"neither finalist 'laik'* on Good Friday as they are still working, unlike the mines"*.

A compromise was reached by playing in the afternoon, rather than the morning, with a higher than usual crowd turning up.

Lionel Smith, aged 19, played for the winners, just four months before signing for Arsenal.

World War Two delayed his Football League debut by almost nine years but he went on to win the title and FA Cup with the Gunners and appeared six times for England.   (* Yorkshire dialect for "play")

Kilnhurst-based Yorkshire Tar Distillers were the 1939 winners. The picture includes Arsenal's Football League and FA Cup winner Lionel Smith and was taken in front of Kilnhurst church. Also pictured, sitting behind the cup, is Jack Burkinshaw, see Family Album section (page 13)

1940-1949

1940
Manvers Main 8
Grimethorpe Rovers 0

The 1940s opened with a bang and a record cup final score.

However, Grimethorpe were handicapped by the loss of one player sent off in the first half and, in the days before substitutes were allowed, another injured in the second.

Rovers did not have to wait long for revenge, beating Manvers Main 5-0 in another competition the following day.

Cyril Grant scored a hat-trick in the Mont final, while Stan Burton also found the net twice. This was a period when many professionals appeared in the competition and 12 months earlier Stan had played in the FA Cup final for Wolverhampton Wanderers in their 4-1 defeat to Portsmouth.

1941
Manvers Main 2
Grimethorpe Rovers 1

A repeat of the previous year's final but this time a much closer encounter, with all three goals coming from headers.

Mark Crook presented the trophy. He went on to form the famous Wath Wanderers, a feeder team for Wolves that gave a platform to players including 1966 World Cup squad members Ron Flowers and Alan Ball, Peter Knowles, Terry Cooper, Alan Sunderland and Steve Daley (see Page 66).

For the second season running, Manvers were quickly brought crashing back to earth – this time beaten 9-1 by Denaby United in a Sheffield Association game later the same day.

The win marked Cyril Warren's third title in three years, having being in Yorkshire Tar Distillers' 1939 team. His son, Sam, won the Mont in 1971, playing for Northcliffe WMC.

The 1940 Manvers Main team and...

... the team with committee members after a third consecutive win in 1942

1942
Manvers Main 4
Upton Colliery 2

Former England schoolboy John Cocker scored a hat-trick as Manvers completed their own Mont treble.

The winning team also included Matt Moralee (Grimsby Town, Aston Villa, Leicester City), Wilf Brown (New Brighton, Rotherham United), Frank Rayner (Mansfield Town, Burnley) and went on to beat Sheffield United Reserves in the Sheffield Challenge Cup final.

1943
New Stubbin Colliery 2 Old Mill 1

South Kirkby side Old Mill went down to goals from Dixon and Perkins (penalty).

1944
Wath Wanderers 2 Denaby United 1 *

Probably the all-time classic Montagu Cup final. The first match ended 3-3 before a record final crowd of 5,704 gathered at Hampden Road for the replay to see two strong sides packed with big names go toe to toe for a mammoth two hours 38 minutes.

Newcastle United and World Cup-bound George Robledo headed Wath into the lead but Wally Ardron equalised from the penalty spot.

It was 1-1 after 90 minutes and it would appear extra time was 'next goal wins'! In the 130th minute Ardron had a penalty saved by Cyril Hannaby (who signed for Hull City one year later) before former Burnley player Frank Rayner headed in

Cyril Warren won a Montagu Cup hat-trick from 1939-1941

Future Hull City goalkeeper Cyril Hannaby saved a penalty for Wath in their 1944 victory. The railway fitter went on to play for Halifax Town and Scarborough, also running a fish and chip shop in Doncaster. He then emigrated to the USA and, while playing for Baltimore, was named League Most Valuable Player in 1954. That same year he guested for Chelsea in an exhibition match against Borussia Dortmund

the winner for Wath 28 minutes later.

The Denaby team included players who had appeared for Leeds United, Newcastle United, Rotherham United, Doncaster Rovers, Leicester City and West Ham United, while the Wath line-up featured players with experience at Wolverhampton Wanderers, Sheffield Wednesday, Burnley and Doncaster Rovers.

During World War Two, teams regularly included players who were allowed to 'guest' for them as well as play for their parent club.

Any club near a military base was guaranteed to attract star names with more than 600 footballers signing up for action.

A busy day for Wally

Wally Ardron scored and then missed a penalty in the 1944 Montagu Cup final for Denaby United.

However, that blot on his record can perhaps be forgiven when you realise what that April 29th day had consisted of...

- 2.15am: Works a train from Mexborough to Cleethorpes as an engine fireman
- 11am: Railway shift ends
- 3pm: Plays and scores in Rotherham United's 1-0 win against Sheffield United at Millmoor
- 6.15pm: Scores in a two hour 38-minute Montagu Cup final

As if that was not enough, Wally travelled between those commitments by bicycle!

Wally still holds the record for the most goals scored in a season for Rotherham United (38) in 1946-47. He holds the same record for Nottingham Forest (36) in 1950-51 and is one of just four players to hold scoring records at two clubs. The others are Jimmy Greaves (Chelsea and Tottenham), Cliff Holton (Northampton and Watford) and Arthur

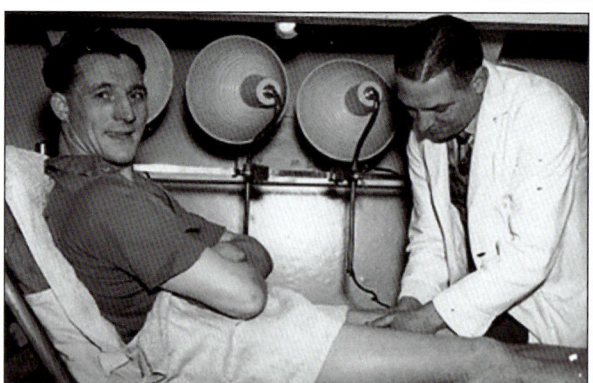

Fit for anything! Denaby's Wally Ardron

Rowley (Leicester and Shrewsbury).

In 1948/49 Wally played for an FA XI against the Army but work commitments stopped him touring with England. Only his move to Forest as a full-time professional enabled him to stop work for the LNER. After retirement from football, he took a job at the steelworks, where his first weekly wage packet was bigger than any of those that he had from a 300-plus game Football League career.

Albert Burrows died in November 2022 at the age of 94 and was the oldest known surviving Mont finalist

Spot the difference. Broomhill Boys' kit was dark blue and, to avoid a clash with the referee's black shirt, a makeshift 'V' was added. Albert Sage used a bandage for his V, which was slightly thicker than his teammates.
Back row, from left: F Depledge, Frudd, Oxley, Sykes, Laye, H Depledge, J Hickling. Middle: Hickling, Mitchell, Sage, Edge, Parkinson, Harvey, Varney. Front: Burrows, T Stevens, Bedford, G Stevens, Woodcock. On ground: Hubbard, Parkinson (mascot), Moreton

Final in focus: 1945

Manvers Main 1 Broomhill Boys 1

Remarkably, this final was settled by a 'next corner wins' rule during extra time.

Albert Burrows remembered that the final was played at Wath Athletic and that the winning corner was conceded at the Bowling Green End. The ground is still there but is now the Moor Road cricket ground.

Due to the war, there were no medals presented – instead, Albert received a "2/6d" saving stamp but was unsure what the winners received.

Malcolm Parkinson's dad Ken told him the Broomhill team struggled to find shirts due to rationing. An appeal to the Broomhill residents for their clothing coupons was almost enough – just one shirt short. The team had to settle for dark blue shirts due to supply shortages in the war.

However, they clashed with the referee's top, so 75-year-old Mrs Bradley had to sew a white 'V' on each one. Unlucky last man Albert Sage had to find his own blue shirt, along with a bandage to help with a makeshift 'V'.

Malcolm also recalled that his dad played in two cup finals that day. After the Mont, he was at Oakwell in the colours of Shipcroft United for the Barnsley Beckett Cup final in the evening.

In the Mont final, Moreton put Broomhill one up and they held on until 10 minutes from full-time when Barlow equalised for Manvers.

Ken remembered they lost when a Manvers player kicked the ball off Edmund Mitchell for a corner.

He also recalled that the final had to kick off early, due to a cricket match taking place on the same ground, which was probably the reason for the corner rule. No reason was given as to why a replay was not considered.

Montagu Cup final programmes of the 1980s mention that the final of 1945 was filmed and a newspaper report ahead of the final confirmed that "further film shots of the match will be made".

However, the only footage to be unearthed is that of the semi-final between Broomhill and Denaby Rovers. It was filmed as part of 'The Great Game' – a film by the British Council aimed at overseas audiences to promote Britain through its favourite game. It is believed the film was shown to the troops in Burma.

The clip is just over a minute long and starts with Cadeby pit, then moves on to Hampden

Albert Burrows gets a trophy during his long playing and refereeing career

A still from the 1945 semi-final video shows the Hampden Road pavilion in the background

Road, Mexborough, where a mock training session is led by Eric Brook and former England manager Frank Buckley.

In 2021, Albert Burrows saw this film for the first time. It is hoped footage of the final will be found so the bizarre conclusion to the final can be seen.

A couple of months after the final, Albert played a first-team match for Halifax Town.

At 94, he was the oldest known surviving Montagu Cup finalist until his death in November 2022. He spent his working life underground at Wombwell Main and Darfield Main collieries.

His appearance for Halifax was as a guest player from Huddersfield Town. He also trained with Barnsley before signing for Boston United. Locally, he played for Miners United and Mitchell & Darfield, going on to be a referee.

Scan this QR code to watch the 1945 semi-final. Alternatively, visit www.montagucup.com/1945-semi-final

The buildings in the background have changed a lot over the last 77 years

Making history: The 1939 FA Cup final

The 1939 FA Cup final included four players from the Don & Dearne district.

One of these, Stan Burton of Wolves, was joined by Arsenal's Lionel Smith in Manvers Main's Montagu Cup final the following year. Stan scored twice in Manvers' 8-0 victory against Grimethorpe Rovers.

Lionel, from Mexborough, had played in the previous year's Mont for Yorkshire Tar Distillers before signing for the Gunners that summer.

Stan was on the losing side in that FA Cup final, as Portsmouth beat Wolves 4-1, with a starting XI that included first goal scorer Bert Barlow

(Kilnhurst), Guy Wharton (Darfield) and Cliff Parker (Denaby), who scored two of the goals, *inset*.

Stan had started his career with Silverwood Colliery, where he worked as a miner.

The 1939 final had even more of a Yorkshire flavour to it, with Portsmouth goalkeeper Harry Walker, born at Aysgarth, and Wolves' Frank Taylor (Hemsworth), also from the Broad Acres.

It was the last FA Cup final before the outbreak of the Second World War, so Pompey have the distinction of being holders longer than any other team – seven years.

Jump Home Guard won the Mont in 1947

Parkgate Welfare with the Mont and Rotherham Charity Cup runners-up shield, which they won in 1948

1946
Kilnhurst Colliery 2
Shipcroft United 1

Billy Deakin and Frank Adey found the net for Kilnhurst but Shipcroft's Woodcock had a real day to forget. He was knocked out when scoring his team's goal.

1947
Jump Home Guard 3
New Stubbin Colliery 2

Frank Horsfield added another goal to his remarkable season's tally with one of Jump Home Guard's treble

It saw him end the season with an incredible 125 goals to his name for the all-conquering side.

1948
Parkgate Welfare 2
Jump Home Guard 1

Jump's hold on the Mont lasted only one year after goals from Dougie Page and Ralph Whitworth sent them to defeat.

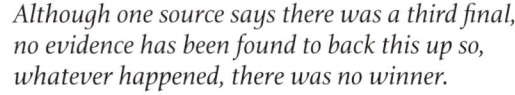
Parkgate Welfare's committee after the club's 1948 victory

1949
Rawmarsh Welfare 1 Kilnhurst Colliery 1 *

The first of two consecutive finals between the same opponents brought a unique record to the competition. Rawmarsh Welfare and local rivals Kilnhurst could not be separated and the trophy was shared for the only time in its history.

Rawmarsh historian Gary Cooper takes up the story:

"In the first match, Charlie Ardron (Wally's brother) scored for Rawmarsh, with George Frith scoring a late equaliser for Kilnhurst in front of 3,600 spectators.

"A second match finished 0-0.

Walt Youren's 1948/9 season Mont winners' medal – the only time the cup was shared

Although one source says there was a third final, no evidence has been found to back this up so, whatever happened, there was no winner.

"The team captains tossed a coin for the right to hold the cup for the first six months. Bill Boden correctly chose 'heads' and Rawmarsh Welfare were presented with the Mont for the first time in their history. When Rawmarsh contacted Kilnhurst after six months to allow them to hold the cup, Kilnhurst secretary Jack Haythorne said that they no longer wanted to share the cup as they claimed that the honour and glory had passed. He did add that they would claim what was rightfully theirs in the 1950 competition."

He was wrong...

Rawmarsh's 1950 trophy successes attracted a large gathering

1950-1959

1950
Rawmarsh Welfare 3
Kilnhurst Colliery 1 *

The saga continued. After two matches failed to separate Rawmarsh and Kilnhurst they were back at Hampden Road a year later and still honours finished even.

Colin Chaplin and Charlie Ardron scored for the 'holders' with Les Harpham and George Frith hitting Kilnhurst's goals in front of 2,528 fans. Step forward Les Swales for the replay nine days later. He scored all three as Rawmarsh won 3-1 to ensure there would be no embarrassing telephone call this time. For good measure, the team also won the Rotherham Charity Cup final, in which Les grabbed another treble.

An unusual report of the first, drawn, 1950 Montagu Cup final

Les Swales' 1950 winners' medal

1951
Rawmarsh Welfare 2
Bowbroom WMC 1

A third two-match final in a row, but this time it was a waterlogged pitch that proved to be the winner in the first encounter.

Les Swales and an own goal from Dawson had seen Rawmarsh 2-1 ahead when heavy rain forced an abandonment just after half time, with the conditions impossible for play to continue – one of only two times the final has been abandoned due to weather conditions in its history (also 1913).

Les scored two more in the re-run to take his tally to six goals in two finals.

1952
Silverwood Colliery 3
Denaby Rovers 0 *

Another year and yet another replay.

The first match was drawn 2-2 but the replay went in favour of Silverwood.

1953
Parkgate Welfare 2
Dragon United 1

A busy two days saw Parkgate Welfare win the Mont and Rotherham Charity Cup on successive days.

It was the first occasion the Montagu Cup had been won at the first time of asking for five years.

1954
Silverwood Colliery 1
Bolton Ings Lane 0

Gordon Rowlands was the Silverwood hero with the only goal of the game in front of more than 3,000 fans back at Hampden Road, after a one year sojourn at Denaby.

Hopes of repeating Parkgate's double were dashed when they were beaten in the Rotherham Charity Cup, in another two-finals-in-two-days event.

1952 Montagu Cup winners Silverwood Colliery

Mrs D Fowler, secretary of the Mexborough Montagu Hospital Comforts Fund, presents the Montagu Cup to Parkgate captain Dougie Page after victory over Dragon United at Denaby United in 1953

Silverwood Colliery's 1954 squad

1956 runners-up Schofield Tech OB

1955: Denaby captain John Roberts takes the Montagu Cup from Mr Griffith, with his team mates and supporters in close attendance

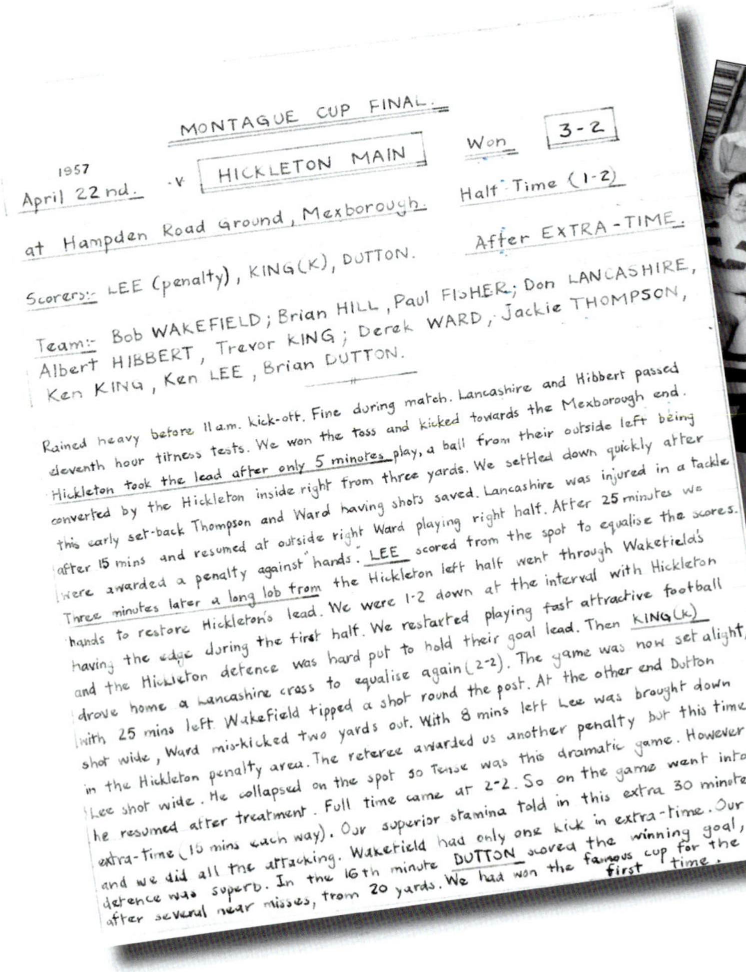

MONTAGUE CUP FINAL.

1957
April 22nd. v HICKLETON MAIN Won 3-2

at Hampden Road Ground, Mexborough. Half-Time (1-2)

After EXTRA-TIME.

Scorers:- LEE (penalty), KING (K), DUTTON.

Team:- Bob WAKEFIELD; Brian HILL, Paul FISHER; Don LANCASHIRE, Albert HIBBERT, Trevor KING; Derek WARD, Jackie THOMPSON, Ken KING, Ken LEE, Brian DUTTON.

Rained heavy before 11 a.m. kick-off. Fine during match. Lancashire and Hibbert passed eleventh hour fitness tests. We won the toss and kicked towards the Mexborough end. Hickleton took the lead after only 5 minutes play, a ball from their outside left being converted by the Hickleton inside right from three yards. We settled down quickly after this early set-back Thompson and Ward having shots saved. Lancashire was injured in a tackle after 15 mins and resumed at outside right Ward playing right half. After 25 minutes we were awarded a penalty against "hands". LEE scored from the spot to equalise the scores. Three minutes later a long lob from the Hickleton left half went through Wakefield's hands to restore Hickleton's lead. We were 1-2 down at the interval with Hickleton having the edge during the first half. We restarted playing fast attractive football and the Hickleton defence was hard put to hold their goal lead. Then KING (K) drove home a Lancashire cross to equalise again (2-2). The game was now set alight, with 25 mins left Wakefield tipped a shot round the post. At the other end Dutton shot wide, Ward mis-kicked two yards out. With 8 mins left Lee was brought down in the Hickleton penalty area. The referee awarded us another penalty but this time Lee shot wide. He collapsed on the spot so Tense was this dramatic game. However he resumed after treatment. Full time came at 2-2. So on the game went into extra-time (15 mins each way). Our superior stamina told in this extra 30 minutes and we did all the attacking. Wakefield had only one kick in extra-time. Our defence was superb. In the 16th minute DUTTON scored the winning goal, after several near misses, from 20 yards. We had won the famous cup for the first time.

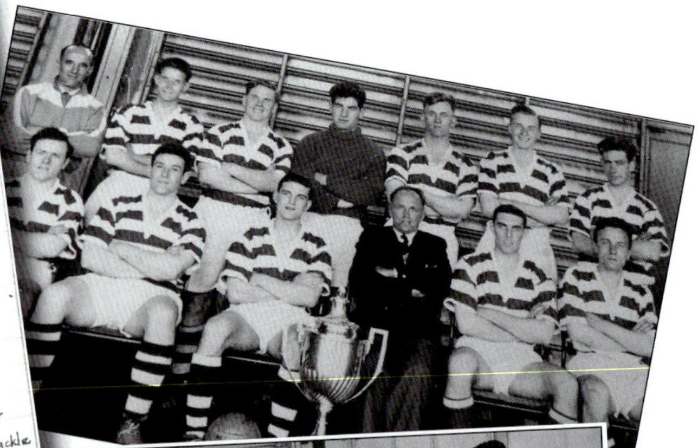

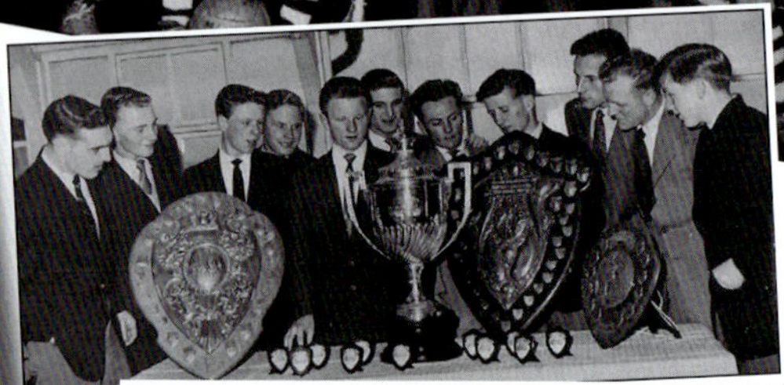

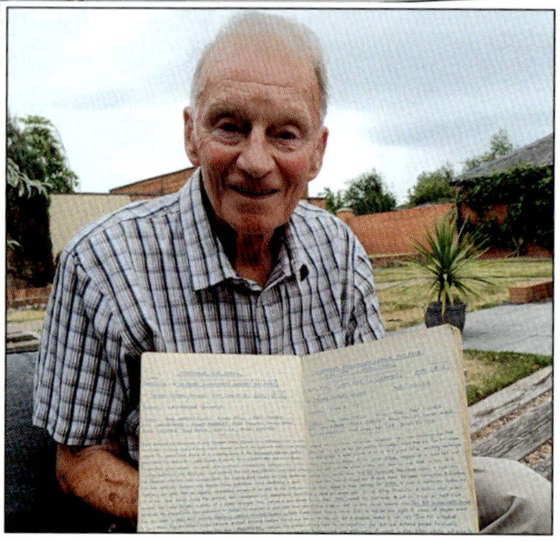

Brian Hill's handwritten match report from the 1957 Mont final. Mexborough Schofield Tech Old Boys, top and centre right, were the winners. Right, Brian with one of his meticulously completed record books.
Read more about Brian Hill's books on page 67

1955
Denaby United 2 Bowbroom WMC 0

A bumper crowd of 4,740 gathered to see Austin and Davies get the goals to earn Denaby United their first Mont since 1915

1956
Dearne CMW 2 Mexborough Schofield Tech OB 1

Back to Denaby for the final, where a brace from Cyril Roebuck proved decisive.

1957
Mexborough Schofield TOB 3 Hickleton Main 2

This match was all about Arnold Atkinson in the build-up. The Hickleton player had postponed his honeymoon in Blackpool to play in the final. Alas, he finished on the losing side. Better news for Derek Ward of the victors though, he had also postponed his honeymoon but managed to keep it out of the papers!

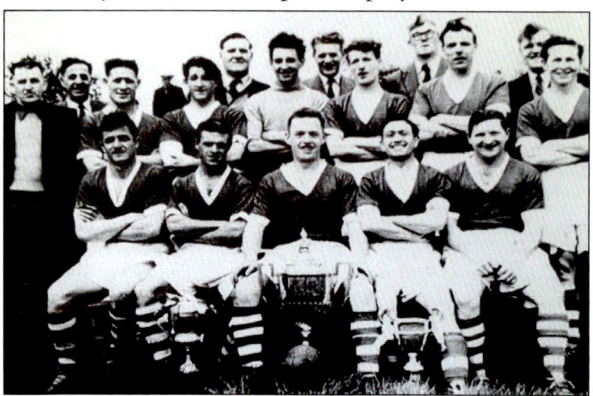

Bowbroom WMC were 1958 winners

1958
Bowbroom WMC 2 Denaby United 0

Rex Trickett played for Bowbroom in this final and, at 93, was the oldest to attend the Meet at the Mont event at the 2022 final.

1959
Tom Hill Old Boys 4 Denaby Rovers 1

Glyn Watkin, Howard Stockwell, Pete Dyson and Richard Marston ensured it was the Old Boys who took the derby honours in an all Denaby final.

Sapey was the Rovers goal scorer.

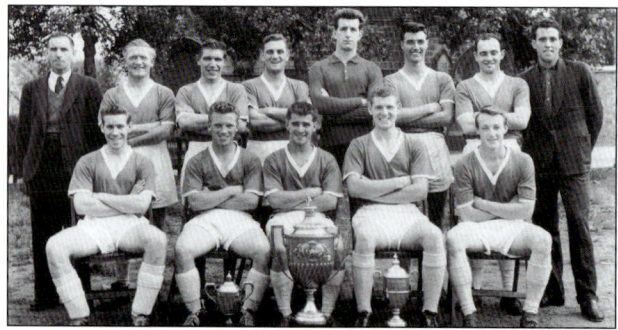

Tom Hill Old Boys beat Denaby Rovers to win an all-Denaby Mont final in front of 3,000 spectators at Hampden Road in 1959

Maltby's 1963 Montagu Cup winners

1966 captains Terry Collinson (High Terrace) and Ben Slade (Maltby)

1960-1969

1960
Ford United 4 Houghton Main 0
The Ford Motor Company had a factory in Balby and Ford United were the factory team. This was the first of Houghton's six final appearances inside 19 years.

1961
Parkgate Welfare 4 Ford United 3
Ford's hopes of retaining the Mont suffered a blow after just 20 minutes when a broken ankle for Tony Rodgers meant they had to play with 10 men.
Even so, Ford were 3-2 up with five minutes to play.

1962
Parkgate Welfare 2 Houghton Main 0
Parkgate made it consecutive Montagu Cup wins after a 30-yard screamer from Terry Staniforth set them on the way to victory.

1963
Maltby MW 5 Tom Hill Old Boys 1
Maltby scored all six goals – five in the right net and one for the opponents.

1964
Swinton Athletic 7 Silverwood Colliery 1
A record-equalling eight-goal final saw Silverwood take the lead through Brian Liversidge. However, their opponents hit back in stunning fashion with Marshall Robshaw getting a hat-trick to take the Mont to Swinton for the first of their record-breaking eight cup wins.

1965
Dearne CMW 3 Maltby Main 1
The Miners' final saw Maltby take the lead before Dearne recovered.

Swinton Athletic captain Brian Hyde receives the Mont in 1964, after the first of the club's eight successes

1966
High Terrace 5 Maltby MW 1 *
The only replayed final of the 1960s after a 2-2 draw, in which the pitch was a quagmire so no extra-time was played.

1967
High Terrace 1 Denaby United 0
High Terrace's double was witnessed by a gate of 3,655 – the highest attendance of the 1960s

1968
Swinton Athletic 2 High Terrace 0
Another bumper crowd saw Swinton prevent a hat-trick for High Terrace. Referee George Albert Flint stopped the game for a lengthy spell to remove spectators from the touchline.

1969
Houghton Main 4 East Dene 2
Substitutes were listed for the first time in a final as Houghton made it third time lucky.

Swinton, and mascot, with the second of their eight Montagu Cups in 1968. Back, from left: Colin Whitehouse (trainer), Melvyn Senior, Paul Kerry, Wilf Winstanley, Ken Whitehead, John Whitehouse, Colin Dawson, Colin Whitehouse, Ken Bradshaw, Eric Johnson. Front: Mick Cooke, Paul Senior, Frank Rix, Brian Hyde, Malc Whitehouse and Billy Walker (treasurer)

Northcliffe Working Men's Club in and out of playing kit with the 1971 Montagu Cup

1970-1979

1970
Denaby United 1
Northcliffe WMC 0 *

The local derby went to a replay after a 0-0 draw in the first match. Kenny Boden crossed for Roger Willey to get the only goal in the replay.

Boden went on to be an international footballer with Australia (see page 63).

Northcliffe's Malcolm Holden was awarded an 'eight-day clock' as man of the match. The clock only needed winding up once a week.

1971
Northcliffe WMC 1
Houghton Main 0

A swift return to the final for Northcliffe and another year when one goal was enough to secure the Mont. George Laycock got the winner against Houghton, who had to play two finals on the same day at the same time.

Swinton's Paul Senior received the Mont after another leap year win in 1972

The League Cup took precedence after a ruling by the County FA and, although they still managed to field a strong side, they were too thinly stretched and were beaten when George's "scorching shot had taken a deflection and hit the underside of the cross bar before entering the net".

Tragedy hit Houghton Main shortly after their 1975 Mont triumph

1972
Swinton Athletic 6 Northcliffe 0

Another leap year and another Swinton win with Malc Whitehouse adding two more goals to the one he got four years earlier. Eighteen-year-old John Wheeler also scored two.

1973
Rawmarsh Horse & Jockey 1 Rawmarsh Welfare 0 *

A real derby final – Horse & Jockey were the 'sister club' of Rawmarsh Welfare according to the South Yorkshire Times:

> "Not only do the clubs share the same ground and many of the same fans, but they also share some of the same players"

In fact, five of the Welfare team could have played for their Sunday League opponents. Jockey were known as Rawmarsh United until shortly before the final. Another low-scoring match saw honours even in the first match at 1-1 before Dave Cousins struck for victory in the replay.

1974
Denaby United 2 Jungle United 1 *

Charles Green was in the Dearne-based Jungle team. He went on to be chief executive at Sheffield United and Rangers.

Frank Morley scored both goals for Denaby in the replay after the first match had ended 1-1.

1975
Houghton Main 3 Northcliffe WMC 2

Houghton Main was one of 18 pits within five miles of Barnsley at the time. A few days after their presentation evening, disaster struck when an explosion in the mine claimed the lives of five men.

Harry Haynes, left, and Tom Gregory, holding the cup, after Houghton's 1975 victory over Northcliffe

1976
Rawmarsh Welfare 3
Swinton Athletic 1

Rawmarsh Welfare won their first trophy for 25 years, ending Swinton's run of leap year victories.

1977
Mexborough Town 2
Edlington WMC 1

Both teams were making their debut in the final.

Ian Smith got one of Mexborough Town's goals. Three years later he scored at Wembley in Mossley's 2-1 FA Trophy final defeat against Dagenham.

1978
Denaby United 4
Houghton Main 2

John Swales made newspaper headlines when he played two matches in one afternoon.

At 3pm he kicked off for BSC Parkgate in the County Senior League and helped his team to a 3-0 half-time lead.

He then dashed to Denaby to play for United in the semi-final of the Montagu Cup in a 4pm kick-off against Northgate WMC.

He came on in the second half and created the only goal in a 1-1 draw.

John Wheeler raises the coveted trophy in 1976 as Rawmarsh Welfare celebrate their first Mont for a quarter of a century

However, a shoulder dislocation later that season resulted in his retirement from football on medical advice when he was just 28 years old.

In the final, Bob Mountain and Allan Craw scored twice each to earn Denaby victory.

1979
Northgate WMC 1 Parkgate 0

Bernard Coop was the hero with the only goal.

He had missed the final the previous year, for Denaby United, because of a broken ankle.

Q. What do Geoff Hurst and Peter Davies have in common?

A. They both scored cup final hat-tricks in 1966!

Peter scored three for High Terrace in their 5-1 replay win against Maltby Miners Welfare. Geoff got his treble in a slightly more widely-publicised cup final played at Wembley Stadium against West Germany.

Northgate's triumphant 1979 team consisted of Lowe, Thacker, S Whitehead, Shepherd, Hardeman, Wrea, B Whitehead, Moore, Coop, South, Walton and substitutes Fogarty and Wren.

1980-1989

1980
Swinton Athletic 3 Edlington WMC 0

A fifth consecutive leap-year final for Swinton and they bounced back from their 1976 defeat in front of more than 3,000 fans at Hampden Road.

1981
Maltby MW 1 Mexborough Main St 0 *

Another low-scoring final with a goal from Richard Moon deciding things in the replay after a goalless first match.

Maltby also won the Rotherham Charity Cup, the first incidence of that particular double since 1953, although it was achieved seven times after that.

1982
Dearne CMW 3 Rotherham Club 1

Rotherham Club were from Swinton, a 1980 merger of the mighty Centralians (County Senior League), who won the Rotherham Charity Cup six times, and Scholes (Rotherham Premier League).

Despite that pedigree, it was Dearne who took the honours.

1983
Mexborough Main Street 2 Northcliffe WMC 0

There were lots of links between these two clubs. Playing on opposite sides were brothers Doug Hemingway (Northcliffe) and John Hemingway (Main Street).

Arthur Roberts presents the 1986 cup to Swinton's Jeff Cooke

Seven of the Northcliffe and four of the Main Street team played for the same Sunday side – Ivanhoe, while former Main Street manager Brian Turton was playing for Northcliffe.

The Winfield and Peart brothers also had split loyalties, with two other pairs of brothers also registered.

Shaun Wilkinson made his debut at just 17 years old. He won it again in 1984 and 1986 – making it three wins within 11 days of his 21st birthday!

He now works for Stelrad – the cup's present sponsor – and presented the trophy in 2020 when his twin sons, Alex and Curtis, were in the winning team. Read more about the Wilkinsons, Page 20.

1984
Mexborough Main Street 2 Goldthorpe Colliery 1

A third of five appearances in seven seasons in the final for Main Street and another winning one.

Doubling up – Rotherham Charity Cup and Montagu Cup winners

There have been 13 instances of a single club winning both the Montagu Hospital Cup and the Rotherham Charity Cup in the same season.

The Rotherham competition started before the Mont, in 1889/90. Money raised from that competition goes to a variety of small, locally-based charities and organisations.

Teams to have done the double are:

1898: Kilnhurst (later declared void)
1906: Wombwell Main
1920: Swinton Discharged Soldiers & Sailors
1950: Rawmarsh Welfare
1953: Parkgate Welfare
1981: Maltby MW
1985: Northgate
2000: Mexborough Main Street

The Rotherham Charity Cup's various trophies

2004: Dearne CMW
2005: Mexborough Main Street
2012: AFP
2014: AFP
2015: Memories

1985
Northgate WMC 3 New Stubbin 0
New Stubbin drew twice with Maltby in the quarter-final before progressing on penalties.

1986
Swinton Athletic 2 Mexborough Main Street 0
Another family affair involving Main Street. Brothers Steve (Swinton) and Michael Coles (Main Street) were in opposition in a final that had been due to be refereed by their father Cyril.

Once the family connections were realised, Cyril's appointment was put back 12 months.

1987
Mexborough Main Street 4 Parkgate 2
Paul Cooke's 25-yarder was the highlight as Main Street made up for the previous year's disappointment.

1988
Denaby & Cadeby 2 Swinton Athletic 1
And so the siblings continue to dominate proceedings. This time three Smith brothers lined up for Denaby & Cadeby – Ian and Gary scored, with Trevor also in the winning line-up.

Denaby & Cadeby's Mark Levers, Steve Watkin and Glenn Hancock in 1988

Swinton's goalkeeper Stuart Lowe was carried off injured after 17 minutes.

1989
Swinton Athletic 2 Wath Saracens 1
After his disappointment of 1988, Swinton goalkeeper Stuart Lowe was back and marked his return with a penalty save. John Hodgson scored a 25 yard 'daisy-cutter' with Don Elliott also finding the way to goal.

Another Montagu Cup for Swinton, this one in 1989

Action from the 1991 Montagu Cup final between Denaby & Cadeby and Swinton Athletic

1990-1999

1990
Goldthorpe Colliery 2
Inferno Fire Protection 0

Inferno Fire Protection (IFP) were formerly the Ring O'Bells at Kimberworth.

Most of the 1,500 strong crowd left after an icy downpour around the hour mark.

Gordon Swann joined 1987 match official Brian Hyde as the only Montagu Cup final referees to have won the trophy as a player.

1991
Denaby & Cadeby 2
Swinton Athletic 1

A late winner decided matters in Denaby & Cadeby's favour.

1992
Brodsworth MW 2
Parkgate 1

A repeat of 12 months earlier with another last-gasp winner.

Long-standing Montagu Cup official Wilf Polhill presents the trophy to Alan Watson, of Wath St James in 1994

1993
Brodsworth MW 2 Goldthorpe Colliery 0 *

Struggling Northern Counties East League side Brodsworth put their poor league season behind them to lift the silverware at the second attempt. The first match at Hampden Road was drawn 1-1 but Gary Cygan and Paul Dodge made no mistake in the replay at Denaby.

1994
Wath St James 1 Goldthorpe Colliery 0

Fifty years after the last Wath winners, St James lifted the Mont thanks to Shaun Temple's goal.

1995
Denaby & Cadeby 2 Mexborough Main Street 0

Another piece of Mont silverware for Denaby manager Wilf Race, who had won the cup three times as a player with Mexborough Main Street.

1996
Denaby & Cadeby 4 Wath Saracens 2

Twice Saracens were winning but Denaby & Cadeby proved too strong as they hit back.

1997
Denaby & Cadeby 2 Wath Saracens 1

A third consecutive win for Denaby & Cadeby in a repeat of the 1997 final.

Again the Wath side took the lead but their opponents struck back and went on to win. It did come at the cost of a booking, however, with Stuart Dudill booked for a 'Ravenelli-style' celebration after scoring – utilising the corner flag.

Paul Cooke played in six Montagu Cup finals and was on the winning side on four occasions. He was captain of Denaby & Cadeby Miners Welfare for their hat-trick (a feat only previously achieved by Hickleton Main 1910-12, Manvers Main 1940-42 and Rawmarsh Welfare 1949-51 – one shared).

Paul had started an 18-month battle to overcome cancer in 1989, involving two operations and four courses of chemotherapy.

Paul Cooke recovered from cancer to lead Denaby & Cadeby to a Montagu Cup hat-trick between 1995-97

1998
Wombwell Main 3 Mexborough Main Street 2

Another comeback victory, this time seeing Wombwell hit back against Main Street.

1999
Mexborough Main Street 1 Denaby United 0 *

Main Street made a swift comeback and this time it was their turn to recover after falling behind, earning a 2-2 draw in the initial staging.

In the replay, former Denaby United player Karl Kent got the winner.

A missed chance for Mexborough Main Street during the 1995 final

Oxer's strike helps Main Street retain Montagu Cup
SUPER SIX FOR GOAL ACE DEAN

Dean Oxer grabbed the 2000 headlines after completing his sixth triumph, this time in the colours of Main Street

2000-2009

2000
Mexborough Main Street 1 Denaby United 0

Dean Oxer celebrated a sixth personal Mont triumph by scoring the only goal of the game.

He had previously won it in 1985 with Northgate, 1989 with Swinton Athletic, and 1995-97 with treble-winning Denaby & Cadeby MW.

2001
Wombwell Main 2 Edlington WMC 0

Edlington replaced Swinton Athletic the week before the final when their opponents refused to continue their semi-final after two players broke legs and two more were sent off.

2002
Wombwell Main 2 Groves Social 1

Pete Smith, at 38 years old, was man of the match.

2003
Wombwell Main 4 Groves Social 2

Three wins on the bounce for Wombwell Main and a repeat of the 2002 final. Wilf Polhill was honoured in the programme.

Wombwell Main's man of the match James Boulton receives his trophy from Sharon Treloar, daughter of former Mont vice-president Wilf Pohill, who had died earlier in 2003

He was one of three men who had run Swinton from their formation and was also a Montagu Cup committee member.

2004
Dearne CMW 6 Westville 1 *

Westville hung on to earn a second bite of the cherry. They scored late equalisers in both the 90 minutes and extra-time to force a replay.

No mistake for Dearne in the replay though with braces for Tom Rae, Scott Clarke and Phil Smith.

A tribute to Montagu Cup vice-president Peter Taylor appeared in the programme. His father, George Albert, won the Mont in 1914 and presented it in 1974. Peter's grand-daughter, Aimee Helliwell, will present the Peter Taylor Memorial Trophy to the 2023 man of the match.

2005
Mexborough Main Street 2 Groves Social 0

A third final in four years for Groves and another defeat. Main Street also won the Rotherham Charity Cup.

Ian Cotton and Dean Oxer with the Mont in 2000 and, right, Richard Portman two years later

Main Street's Gary Hibbert scores from the spot but his team were beaten by Wombwell Main in the 2007 final

CUP WIN LEAVES MAIN IN SEVENTH HEAVEN

Mexborough Main Street's captain Mark Nisbett proudly kisses the Montagu Cup that they won in the match on Monday. Picture: Holly Allen.

by Liam Hoden
at Hampden Road
liam.hoden@dearnetoday.co.uk

**MONTAGU CUP FINAL
DEARNE CMW 0
MEXBOROUGH MAIN STREET 3**

MAIN made it into seventh heaven as they captured the Montagu Cup in a highly competitive contest on a bitingly cold and windswept Easter Monday at Hampden Road.

The win gave John Mighali's side their seventh triumph in the 111-year-old competition and their first for three years as their killer touch proved the difference in a midfield war of attrition between two County Senior League sides.

After scraping past The Cottage and Swinton WMC on penalties and beating Westville in the semi final, Main enjoyed a relatively easier time of it against 2004 winners Dearne CMW and lifted the South Yorkshire Times-sponsored trophy.

Midfielder Adam Hallsworth opened the scoring as the quarter hour mark approached before dead ball specialist Chris Greaves increased the cushion with a superb free kick five minutes later.

Much of the first half play was bogged down in midfield with both sides exchanging blows but providing little in the way of decent chances.

Main appeared to settle into the conditions easier than their opponents and their crisp passing play gave them the edge over their opponents, who largely struggled throughout the morning.

Dearne did emerge from the break with their tails up and began to take the game to Main but soon settled back into their first half form.

Five minutes in, it was Main who should have increased their lead but a wayward free header and a pulled shot denied them the opportunity of sealing the game.

It was not long before they were three up, however, as referee Brian Hardeman awarded a penalty to Main.

A long ball into the box found Ryan Tate who controlled well and advanced before going down under a challenge.

Despite heavy protests, the spot kick was given and Rob Branagan stepped up confidently to send the keeper the wrong way and add to his lower-than-normal goal tally this season.

Neither side particularly impressed throughout the contest and the rest of the game played out with the odd chance here and there but both defensive lines should be praised for their resolute performances in difficult conditions.

Andrew Joburns between the Mexborough sticks proved to be Dearne's tormentor as he denied them on several occasions including an excellent save in a one on one situation.

His opposite number Lee Gray had his share of the action when Main enjoyed a five minute period camped in the final third.

Gray demonstrated his fantastic reactions as he pulled off an unbelievable save when the ball was fired at him from point blank range and the big man should also be commended for diffusing a fiery confrontation as tempers and frustrations flared.

Dearne really should have had a consolation strike late on when an excellent cross from the right was met well but turned narrowly wide and ensured a clean sheet for Main.

● For more photos from the Montagu Cup final, see our website www.southyorkshiretimes.co.uk/sport

A report about the 2008 Mont final from the South Yorkshire Times

2006
Conyers 3 Houghton Main 0 *

Anthony Storey's late equaliser for Houghton ensured a 1-1 draw and a replay.

The programme contained tributes to Alan Cliff, Montagu Cup secretary, 1984-2003, and Denis Townsend, the treasurer, who had recently died.

2007
Wombwell Main 5 Mexborough Main Street 1 *

Main Street fought back to draw 2-2 in the first match but Wombwell were too strong in the replay.

2008
Mexborough Main Street 3 Dearne CMW 0

Main Street made up for the previous year's disappointment with victory in the South Yorkshire Times-sponsored cup.

2009
Wombwell Main 4 Westville 0

The South Yorkshire Times provided a comprehensive programme for a final that saw punches 'thrown and landed' in a match where two players were sent off. Tribute was paid to Derrick Jones, the Mont president, who had been involved in Mexborough football for 50 years.

Reece Wesley of AFP with the 2012 Mont after a single goal was enough to beat Swinton Working Men's Club

2011 winner Ian Beardsley and, inset, 2015 manager Shaun Needham

2010-2019

2010
Groves Social 2 Wombwell Main 1

The South Yorkshire Times produced an excellent programme again for a match that was goalless until the second half of extra-time.

The referee was 28-year-old Matt Bacon, who is now (2022) on the brink of becoming a Football League match official, currently on the National League line.

2011
Swinton WMC 2 Houghton Main 1

The first time the Mont was won by a Swinton team for 22 years.

2012
AFP 1 Swinton WMC 0

Andrew Haythorne scored in the 118th minute to wrap up the cup.

2013
AFP 2 Swinton WMC 0

Man of the match Paul Gratton saved a Swinton penalty before AFP triumphed with nine men against 10.

Photographer Ben Webster got some cracking pictures of the 2015 final

2014
AFP 1 Swinton Athletic 0
Three Monts on the bounce for AFP and all against Swinton opponents. Rob Branagan equalled the individual record by playing in his seventh final.

2015
Memories 4 Swinton Athletic 3
Memories came back from 3-1 down to win 4-3. Their manager Shaun Needham watched as his son, Tommy, scored the winner in the last minute of extra-time. (See Page 15)

2016
AFP 3 Houghton Main 1
Four wins in five seasons for AFP equalled Hickleton Main's achievement of more than 100 years earlier (1908-1912).

2017
Houghton Main 1 Joker 0
A first win for Houghton Main since 1975, having finished as runners-up four times since then.

A goal in extra-time by Danny Burkinshaw was the difference.

2015: Ben Webster captures a goal, top, and the watching crowd, above

Memories won 4-3 after being 3-1 down in the 2015 final. Tommy Needham got the winner. Pictured Danny South (No.9) after scoring a direct free-kick for Memories

2018
Westville 4 Wombwell Main 0

Westville won the Mont for the first time, and in convincing fashion.

2019
Joker 6 Wombwell Main 0 *

Four goals from Ross Duggan and a brace from Steve McDonnell helped Joker to crown an outstanding season.

The winning margin equalled the post-war record set by Swinton Athletic.

The final was re-staged after the first match was abandoned following a double leg-break suffered by Joker's Gary Podmore before half-time.

Joker were 2-0 up thanks to a goal from Ryan Smyth and Dan Patterson's penalty before chaotic scenes after the injury led to three dismissals for Wombwell Main.

Ross Duggan's four goals in the second match equalled Sid Dawson's 1914 record for the highest number of goals scored in a Montagu Cup final.

The wait was over for Houghton Main in 2017, top

Laughs all round for 2018 winners Westville, left

2020-2022

2020
Swinton Athletic 5 Westville 2

Coronavirus looked like interrupting a 102-year run of Montagu Cup finals. Eventually, thanks to secretary Barrie Dalby and the committee, the final was played in August behind closed doors at Queens United's ground in West Melton.

Curtis Wilkinson's 30-yard strike into the top corner of the net for Swinton's fifth goal was caught on video in another high-scoring encounter.

Watch the final highlights on YouTube, thanks to FC NonLeagueFootball here – https://tinyurl.com/curtiswilkinson

The Montagu Cup and individual mementoes ahead of the 2021 presentation

2021
Swinton Athletic 2 Joker 1

Swinton Athletic clinched a record-breaking eighth success.

Shawn Mitchell played in his seventh Montagu Cup final and, even more notably, collected his third man of the match award (2018 and 2019 were the others).

Joker had beaten AFP on penalties in the semi-final after an entertaining 3-3 draw.

2022
Scawthorpe Athletic 4 Dog Daisy United 3

Les Payne's match report for the Doncaster Free Press summarised a goal-laden final in perfect style.

"It was a day and a final to match the occasion and it is almost certain that in its 125 years, the Mexborough Montagu Cup has never seen a final quite

Swinton Athletic celebrate their history-making eighth Montagu Cup win. Inset, the Bernard Hodgkinson Memorial Shield, which is presented to the competition runners-up

Scawthorpe Athletic and Dog Daisy United line up for the historic 125th Montagu Cup final

like this one. Firstly, has one team ever scored three times in the first TEN minutes – as Dog Daisy United did here? Highly unlikely.

And as there had only ever been three 4-3 scorelines in a Mont final before this one, this is almost certain to be the first time a team has come from 3-0 down to win the coveted trophy – as Scawthorpe Athletic did on Easter Monday and for the first time.

It proved a tremendous game for a crowd that must have topped 1,700 after the day started perfectly when over a hundred former Mont finalists from across many decades flocked into the Mexborough Athletic club to meet old pals and reminisce, making it a great start to the 125th anniversary.

Josh Moore opened the scoring after four minutes, with Jake Ford notching a swift double after six and 10 minutes to put Dog Daisy seemingly well on the way to victory.

However, Lee Tilley struck after 33 minutes to make it 3-1 at the break and second-half goals from Scawthorpe's Adam Watson and Gaz Mundy made it 3-3 at full-time before Sam Corner struck a 109th-minute winner to complete a stunning comeback.

Goalmouth action from Scawthorpe's stunning comeback

> The Mont has never been won on penalties. There have been many final replays but the rules now state the final shall be decided on penalties if teams are level after extra-time. This has not been needed – yet!

A bumper crowd for the 2022 staging of the Mont

More Montagu Cup final 2022 action. Top, Dog Daisy on the attack; above left, Sam Corner, who scored Scawthorpe's extra-time winner; above top, a touchline tangle; above bottom, Scawthorpe's Lee Tilley pulled one back before half-time and, below, groundsman Steve Poole's handiwork

RADIATING HISTORY...

Stelrad Radiators has been manufacturing radiators since 1936 and it's fascinating to see how it has encouraged heating engineers and plumbers to choose Stelrad radiators rather than its competitors, through the decades. Here we have reproduced a selection of advertisements the company has used to raise awareness of the products it has manufactured, with a range of features and benefits that might persuade readers to opt for these models.

These are just a few of the historic advertisements that the company has in its archives. Today's marketing activities are considered more specialised and scientific than these relatively simple advertisements were in their day. So, whilst the company still places advertisements in the relevant trade media, its marketing reaches across a vast array of opportunities. Not just the print media as in the early days, but in an array of digital and online media, ensuring Stelrad tells its story as far and wide as possible through every potential outlet that will be seen by those responsible for specifying and buying radiators across the UK and Ireland.

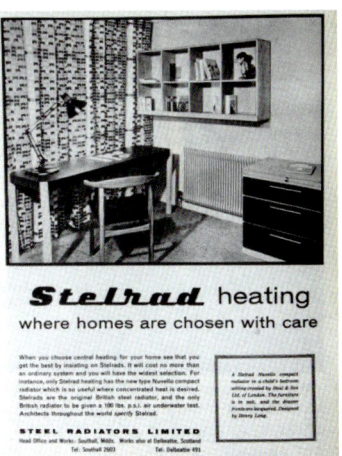

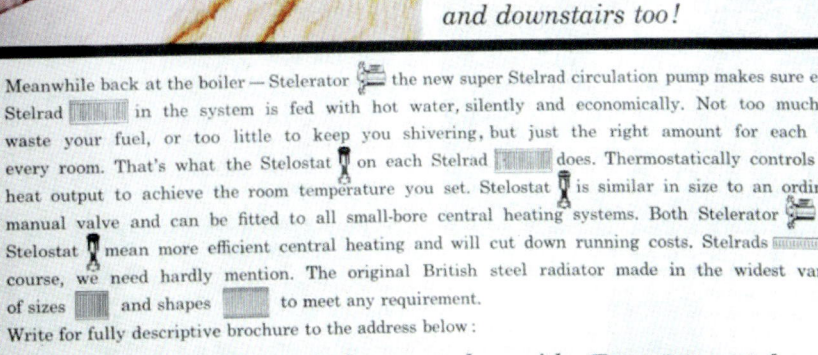

Meet at the Mont

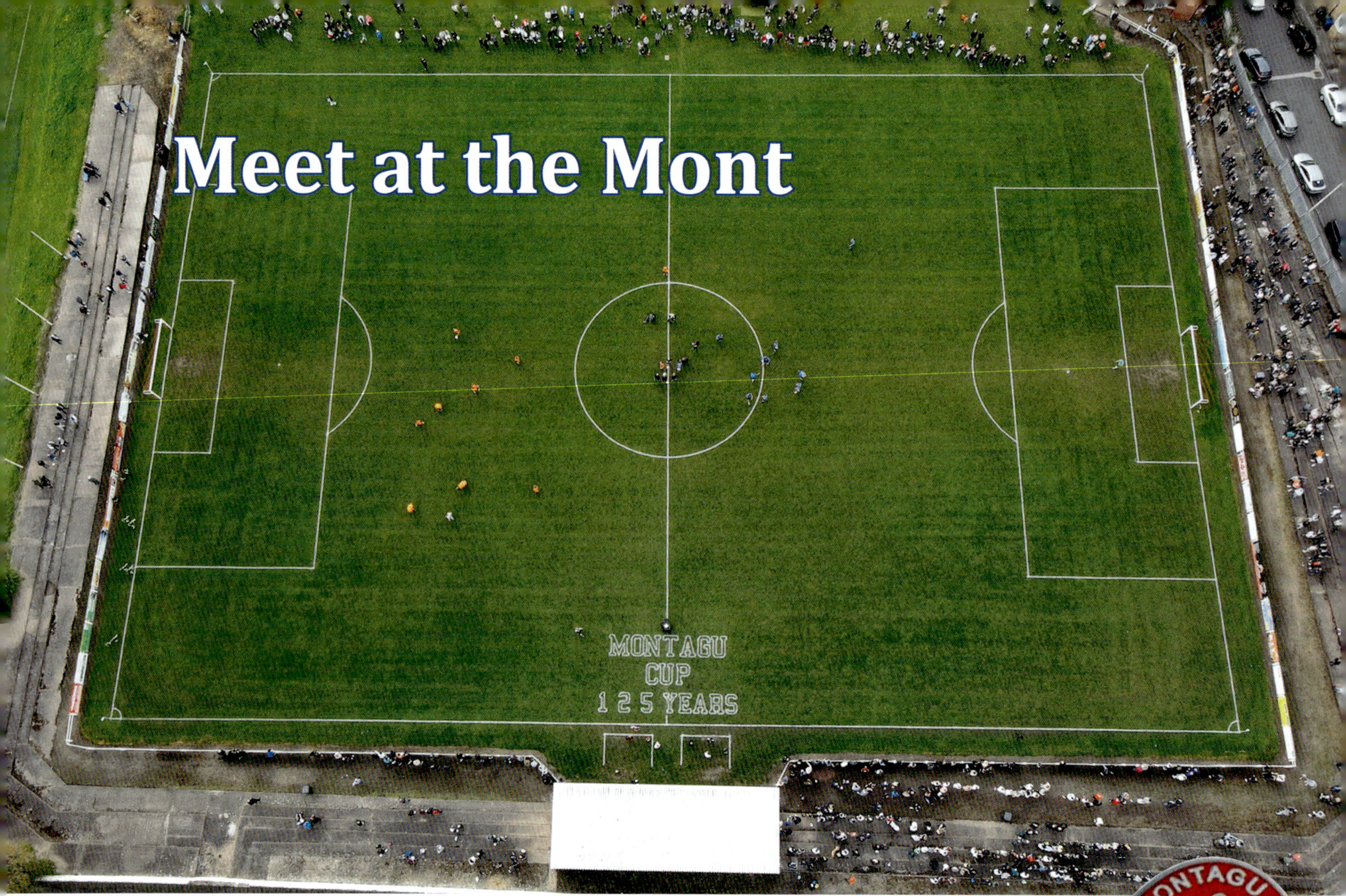

An aerial view of the Hampden Road ground, home of Montagu Cup finals since 1897

On Easter Monday 2022, 125 years of the Mexborough Montagu Hospital Charity Cup were celebrated with a Meet at the Mont event for past finalists and their descendants.

Many attendees wore commemorative pin badges to mark the occasion.

Guests arrived at the Athletic Club at 9am for a brew and photographs before watching the thrilling Montagu Cup final at 11am.

Elizabeth Robledo travelled from Chile to represent her father, George

Montagu Cup finalists, families and officials gather to mark the 125th anniversary of the competition

Robledo, who scored in the 1944 final.

Brian Hill made a special trip from Bournemouth to be at the reunion. He played for Mexborough Schofield Tech Old Boys in the 1956 and 1957 Montagu Cup finals.

Paul Hyde (winner 1986 and 1989): "We saw many old faces and had a good catch up. That sort of thing doesn't happen too often. The final did justice to the Montagu Cup and fitted in with the celebrations beautifully – a great advert for the Mont."

David Whitworth (supporter): "Genuinely appreciate the time and effort so many people put in to make the anniversary so special. It meant so much to Brian (Hill) and Walt (Taylor, four-time winner) and the opportunity for me to share it with them."

Brian Hill (Mexborough OB reunion coordinator): "Easter Monday 2022 was a special and memorable occasion."

Wilf Race (seven-time winner): "A wonderful event and I met some lovely people."

John Hobson (photographer): "It was a pleasure to work it yesterday. Boy did I meet some interesting characters! My favourite... probably "Wacka" (John Smith, 1975 winner) ... I had a right conversation with him!"

To view more pictures from the Meet at the Mont day, visit the following websites:
www.montagucup.com/meet-at-the-mont
johnhobsonphotographer.co.uk/meet-at-the-mont/
tinyurl.com/Mont2022

Meet at the Mont offered the chance to pose with the famous trophy

Trivia

First Englishman to manage a World Cup final team

Wombwell-born George Raynor can stake a genuine claim to be the most successful English international manager there has ever been.

Although no evidence has been found of him playing in the Mont, he was with several clubs who did compete in it at a similar time to when he was with them, including Wombwell, Mexborough Athletic and Elsecar Bible Class.

After a brief Football League career that took in Sheffield United, Mansfield Town, Rotherham United, Bury and Aldershot, George made his name as Sweden national team manager. He led them to gold at the 1948 Olympic Games in London and two years later, despite the Swedish FA banning the national team from using professionals, saw them finish third in the World Cup in Brazil.

1952 saw him pick up a bronze Olympic medal in Helsinki, Finland, before moving to manage Italian giants Juventus in 1954 and later Lazio. George was back in charge of Sweden in 1958 and steered his team to the final, where they were beaten by a Brazil team that included Pele.

He was the first Englishman to reach a World Cup final but found a job in English football hard to find. A few months after the World Cup final he accepted a job as manager of non-League Skegness Town. He retired not long after, returning briefly to manage Doncaster Rovers in 1967/68.

George was knighted in Sweden but is barely remembered in England.

- Jagger Holling scored in consecutive finals – 1899 and 1901 – with two different winning teams. There was no Mont played in 1900.

 In the first he netted twice for Mexborough in a 3-1 win against Wath and two years later was on target in Doncaster Rovers' 5-2 win against Mexborough Thursday.

- 1902 Denaby United finalist Tim Roper had fought in the Boer War. It was a conflict fought from 1899 to 1902 between the British Empire and the two Boer Republics (the South African Republic and the Orange Free State).

- South Kirkby did not have a lot of luck in Mont finals. In 1906 F Hough gave away a penalty and then later missed one in a 2-1 defeat to Wombwell Main, decided by an own goal from Powers. A year earlier, Kirkby had also lost to the only goal of the game, scored by Christopher Crapper into his own net against Mexborough Town.

- Willis Rippon scored seven of the nine goals that secured the Montagu Cup for Kilnhurst in 1907, including one in the final against Parkgate & Rawmarsh. After the final, councillor John Clayton presented and filled the Mont with a gallon of port. This half filled the trophy and he said he hoped his teetotal friends would not find fault with his actions.

- In the first drawn 1911 final between Hickleton Main and Ryecroft Wesleyans, a supporter annoyed the newspaper reporter by playing his melodian.

- Mexborough Grand Central Loco's 1915 semi-final took three matches to decide. The final, which they lost to Denaby United, also took three matches to find a winner.

- In 1920, the Sheffield & Hallamshire FA agreed to allow a seven-mile radius as the area of the competition for the Montagu Hospital Cup.

- In 1919 a Montagu Shield competition was started for schools. Initially this was played for on Easter Tuesday. The competition ran until 1970.

 The shield is now in the West Melton home of David Kitchen.

- A 1921 report of the final mentions an attack towards the secondary school end. This indicates that the pitch was at 90 degrees to the present orientation.

- The Montagu Cup final was played on Good Friday throughout the 1920s and 1930s.

- Jack Selkirk played for Ford United in the 1960 and 1961 finals, having previously made 452 appearances at right back for Rotherham United.

Burnley's best

Hoyland's Tommy Boyle was described as a great header of the ball and an excellent passer with great leadership qualities. He was widely recognised as one of the best players ever to play for Burnley.

Having lifted the FA Cup in 1914, he became the first Burnley captain to lift the Football League Championship trophy when Burnley won the 1920/21 title.

Tommy had served as a gunner in the Royal Field Artillery during World War One and was wounded in 1917.

After retiring from playing, Tommy worked as a landlord, but was committed to a psychiatric hospital in 1930. He died at Whittingham Hospital, Lancashire, 10 years later, and was buried in an unmarked grave in Hoyland.

Players

Some of the characters, record breakers and big names who have a proud Montagu Cup pedigree

Kenny Boden in action on the other side of the world after his move to Australia

Kenny Boden

In the 1970 Montagu Cup final, Denaby United's 20-year-old Kenny Boden set up an 88th-minute winner for Roger Willey. Within nine years he was playing international football for Australia.

That came after a whirlwind career for the painter and decorator, which also took in stints with Joker FC, Hull City, Scunthorpe United, Sheffield United, Gainsborough Trinity, Matlock Town, Bridlington Trinity, Brigg Town and one Football League match for Doncaster Rovers.

He emigrated Down Under in 1978 and played for Newcastle KB United, Sydney City, Sydney City Slickers and Sydney Croatia. He finished with a professional career total of 68 goals in 167 games.

Kenny made a swift impression because he was called up by the Socceroos to play in an exhibition match against a New York Cosmos team that included Franz Beckenbauer. The Oz side won 1-0 and Kenny went on to make 13 full appearances for the national side, including a 1980 clash with an England team that included Glenn Hoddle and Bryan Robson. One of his other caps came in a crunch World Cup 1982 qualifier against New Zealand. He played in a 3-3 away draw but was injured for the decisive second leg, which the hosts lost 2-0.

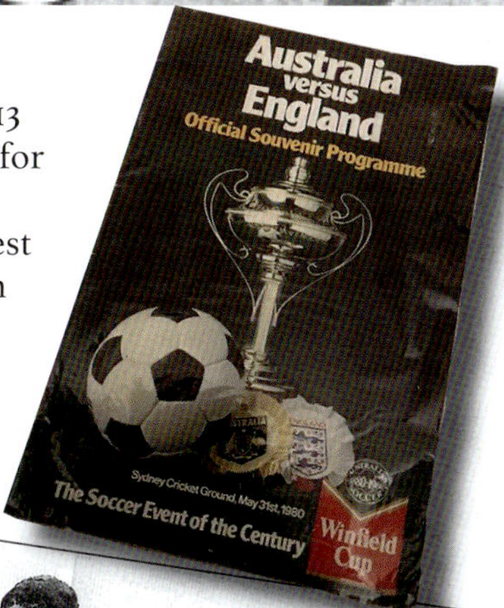

Kenny also played 13 times at other levels for his adopted country and was voted the best player in Australia in the 1978 season, in which he was the league's top scorer.

His KB United

team mate for one match was Bobby Charlton, who was amazed to find an English player with so much skill who had failed to make his name in the UK.

Kenny moved to Sydney City for a £30,000 national record transfer fee and helped them to a league title treble in 1980, 81 and 82.

Kenny is now enjoying retirement in Perth, Australia, where he finished his playing days at local level aged 40.

The lad from Thrybergh who became the wizard of Oz

Kenny Boden went from humble beginnings in Rotherham Sunday football to become Australia's Player of the Year and rub shoulders with some of the game's best. **DAVID BEDDOWS** looks back at his remarkable career

HE was born in Thrybergh, became a stand-out talent in local football and then made a name for himself on the other side of the world.

Kenny Boden's journey from Sunday football with Joker FC to starring for the Socceroos and in club football in Australia is Roy of the Rovers stuff.

While in Australia he played against England, managed to get the better of the great Franz Beckenbauer, and in 1978 became the National Soccer League's Player of the Year.

A painter and decorator by trade, Kenny weaved beautiful patterns on the pitch, his skills so good that Bobby Charlton once asked him: "Where have you been hiding?"

Kenny started his football career with Denaby United in the late 1960s and won the Mexborough Montagu Cup with them in 1970.

His dad knew Rotherham United ace Wally Ardron, who had played for Denaby, and asked Denaby to give him a trial.

Alongside his Saturday football Kenny turned out for Joker, then still a young club starting to make its mark in grassroots football.

He soon began to forge a reputation in Joker's Rotherham Sunday League side and then the Midlands Sunday League in which each week they went up against the best amateur teams in the region.

"Nobody could handle him," remembers Eddie Green, club secretary at the time who first asked Kenny to join them.

"You couldn't keep count of his goals — one, two three, four. He only needed a sniff. He was so deadly."

His thoughts were echoed by committee man Brian Rodgers.

"If a team is wasting time, it will take the ball into the corner. We didn't. We gave it Kenny because the other team never got the ball back.

"I have never seen football played at our level with the skill and input he had."

Playing football on Saturdays and Sunday and with a full-time job as a painter and decorator, life was good for Kenny and it didn't make sense financially to turn full-time pro, even though there was interest.

His coach at Joker was Mick Hennigan, another Thrybergh lad who would go on to coach in the Football League, most famously as assistant to Howard Wilkinson when Leeds United won the old First Division 30 years ago.

Kenny followed Mick to Matlock Town and to Gainsborough Trinity and when he was sacked,

NATIONAL STAR ... Kenny Boden (circled) with the Australian national team around 1980 and (below) in action for Newcastle KB United. Right: match programme from the Australia v England game he played in.

> **Nobody could handle him. He only needed a sniff. He was so deadly.**

International class

Some of the players who gained international honours from in and around the Don/Dearne area

- 31: George Robledo (b1926) West Melton, 8 goals
- 26: Ernest Blenkinsop (b1902) Cudworth
- 20: Wilf Copping (b1909) Houghton
- 20: Eric Brook (b1907) Mexborough, 10 goals
- 13: Kenny Boden (b1950) Thrybergh, 2 goals
- 11: Jack Barker (b1906) Denaby
- 9: Ted Robledo (b1928) West Melton
- 8: Mark Crossley (b1969) Hoyland
- 6: Lionel Smith (b1920) Mexborough
- 4: Willie Watson (b1920) Bolton on Dearne (plus 23 Test matches)
- 4: Fred Tilson (b1904) Swinton, 6 goals
- 3: Gordon West (b1943) Darfield
- 3: Sam Cowan (b1901) Swinton
- 2: Walter Bennett (b1874) Mexborough
- 2: Tommy Boyle (b1886) Hoyland
- 1: George Utley (b1887) Elsecar
- 1: Arthur Willis (b1920) Denaby
- 1: Alan Sunderland (b1953) Conisbrough
- 1: Jimmy Sayer (b1862) Mexborough

WITH DUNLOP
THE GAME'S AT YOUR FEET

KENNY BODEN WEARS

DUNLOP SPORTS FOOTWEAR

Kenny was shining light in Joker side

HE may now be on the other side of the world in Australia, but Kenny Boden left behind a raft of happy memories and admirers from his time with Rotherham Sunday side Joker.

The attacker starred for them in the 1970s in an era when the Bramley side included other top players like Barry Bates, Dave Parlett and Colin Walker.

"When he first came into the group, he was training at the gymnasium at Thrybergh School," said committee member Brian Rodgers. "He was 15 when he was introduced by his school PE teacher. He said 'let this lad have a run around with you.' I could recognise his skill even more on a five-a-side gymnasium pitch."

Joker secretary Eddie Green said Kenny "never batted an eyelid" when he asked him to join them and soon hit his stride in his four years with the club.

He added: "We once played Perry Barr at Birmingham. We played five ringers, including Alan Ogden, who played in the first division for Sheffield United, but all people were asking about was Kenny.

"One year we entered the FA Sunday Cup and we went to play against Rochdale Hornets. After the match their manager came in to shake Kenny's hand and he said: 'You're the best player I've ever seen, kid.'"

Eddie also had some very personal marks to show for Kenny's skill.

"In one match I had to play up front," he said. "I caught the ball on my chest. I couldn't get it down and Kenny volleyed it straight off my chest and into the back of the net. He left burn marks!"

Scouts from Football League clubs were regularly at Joker games but making a switch just wasn't lucrative enough in those days.

"Kenny got money for playing on Saturday, a few bob from us for Sundays and had his full time job as a painter and decorator with Pecks. He was alright as he was," added Eddie.

FOND MEMORIES ... Eddie Green.

Boden moved to Bridlington Trinity and had a trial with Doncaster Rovers.

At the same time, the seeds of his move to Australia were being sown.

Kenny remembers: "The next season started badly for Bridlington, the manager was dismissed and the new guy was called Mick Jones. Mick had been coaching in Australia and he told me that at the end of the season he was going back to coach there and asked me if I fancied playing in Australia."

When the next season started, Kenny had signed for Brigg Town in the Midland League.

"We were by far the best team and by Christmas we had virtually won the league," said Kenny.

"Then one cold day in Rotherham a guy called Alan Vest (player coach from Newcastle KB United in Sydney) knocked on my door and asked me if I fancied playing for them."

Still in his 20s, Kenny didn't need asking twice to pack his bags and board the plane.

"I was to sign a two-year contract," he said. "They would fly my wife, Shirley, and myself over there and after two years would fly us back."

A clutch of other Joker players were also invited Down Under but it was Kenny who settled and made a new life there.

"When the season started, we lost 5-1 and there were 15,000 spectators there," he said.

"As the season went on Newcastle improved and so did I."

In his two seasons with KB, Kenny scored 26 goals in 52 games, including 14 in that first campaign, earning the Player of the Year award. Bobby Charlton made an appearance that season.

Kenny became a big name, drawing the best crowds in Australia to KB's International Sports Centre ground.

Newcastle KB United footballing doyen Ray Baartz said: "You see players that come out here who've played at a higher level and they don't adjust. I guess Kenny was just the perfect fit.

"He was a super player. Every time he got involved you would anticipate something happening, whether that was scoring a goal or beating a man."

It was when Kenny started his second season well, still scoring plenty of goals, when his chance to play for Australia came.

"The new coach of the Socceroos came to watch one of our home games," he said. "Afterwards he asked me whether I would be available to play some friendlies for the Socceroos.

BOBBY CHARLTON recognised Kenny Boden's talent and Franz Beckenbauer (below) finished up on the losing side against him.

"Our first was against New York Cosmos and the team was full of great players, including one guy called Franz Beckenbauer. We managed to beat them 1-0.

"Then we played against England in Sydney. Bryan Robson, Glenn Hoddle and Alan Sunderland were in the England team and we lost 2-1. I managed to swap shirts with Alan Sunderland."

Boden's Australian adventure led to him becoming naturalised and playing in 26 games for the Socceroos, including 13 full internationals and a crucial qualifier against New Zealand for the 1982 World Cup to be held in Spain.

"Our first game was away and we drew it 3-3," said Kenny. "The second game was on the Sydney cricket ground and I couldn't play because I was injured. We lost 2-0 which meant New Zealand (coached by Kevin Fallon from Bramley) went to the World Cup."

By that time, Kenny's two years at Newcastle had come to an end, the club forced to sell him due to financial pressures.

"I was offered a four-year contract by Sydney City," said Kenny. "They'd come second in the league and offered a £30,000 transfer fee, which was the highest in Australia at the time.

"I started my time in Sydney very well. We won the league in 1980, 1981 and 1982."

At the end of 1984 Kenny moved from Sydney and spent five years playing for Perth before finally hanging up his boots.

Now aged 71, he still lives there to this day.

Future Liverpool ace shared flight

KENNY BODEN shared a flight to Australia with a certain Craig Johnston.

The two played together at Newcastle KB United in Sydney and Johnston eventually went on to enjoy a brilliant career back in England, most notably with Liverpool.

Years later, a TV poll of the most successful players from British shores to play in Australia placed Rotherham's Boden top, ahead of the likes of Johnston, Ralph Coates and Emile Heskey.

Thanks also to Phil Roddis and Chris Brook in the compilation of this feature.

Kenny Boden tells his story to David Beddows *Feature courtesy of Rotherham Advertiser*

Allan Craw in his playing days and more recently

Allan Craw

Allan scored two goals in Denaby United's 1978 Montagu Cup final victory over Houghton Main. He had previously won the cup with Rawmarsh Horse & Jockey in 1973. He scored in both semi-finals on the way to those finals.

He recalled one of his earliest football lessons: "I was young, playing with a football in the garden at my mum and dad's house in the Canyon at Rawmarsh. Our next-door neighbour Jimmy Miller* said to me that if I wanted to be a good footballer, I should learn to kick with both feet.

"So from that day on I used to practise kicking the ball with my left foot into the goal. Although I didn't play professionally, I did play in a good standard with Rawmarsh Welfare and Denaby United in the Yorkshire League and Mexborough Town in the Midland League. We did get paid expenses, so I suppose it was as a part-time professional.

"The two goals I scored in the 1978 final were with my left foot so I had to thank Jimmy Miller for his advice all those years before as it helped me throughout the time I played football from 1966 to 1989."

(* Jimmy's son Peter had won both a Montagu Cup winner's medal in 1961 and a Rotherham Charity Cup winner's medal in 1960 with Parkgate Welfare.)

Mark Crook

Mark Crook's Wath Wanderers was an academy for Wolverhampton Wanderers

Former Wolves player Mark ran a young side behind Cortonwood Welfare Club in Brampton Bierlow and fed promising youngsters from the North and North East to Molineux.

Legendary Wolves manager Stan Cullis wrote in his 'All for the Wolves' book, published in 1960:

Wanderers' Mark Crook

"Wath is probably the first football club ever formed for the primary purpose of finding outstanding youngsters to pass on to a parent organisation and it is almost worth its weight in gold.

"The idea formed in the lively brain of Mark Crook, the Wolves winger of the 1930s, who bought a fish-shop when he retired to Yorkshire just before the war.

"His interest in football led him to spot two local lads – Colin Collindridge and Gerald Henry – who he brought to Molineux for a trial.

"Major Buckley did not sign either, although Collindridge later became a successful player for Sheffield United and Nottingham Forest while Henry enjoyed many good seasons with Leeds United.

"Mark thought it would be a good thing if he could keep the promising youngsters for coaching and training until he was sure they reached the high standards the Major demanded.

"So, in 1938, he formed his own club, called Brampton Welfare, and not many years went by before he was finding youngsters who were to become some of the top names in football.

"Both George and Ted Robledo, the brothers who were born in Chile and later earned FA Cup winners medals with Newcastle United, were among his early recommendations and, indeed, as a 15-year-old, in 1942, George scored two goals for Wolves in a charity match at Merthyr.

"War conditions made it difficult to sign youngsters from a distant part and the two Robledos went to Barnsley, who later sold them to Newcastle for a big fee.

"Now, Wath put out two teams each Saturday, one in the Northern Intermediate League and the other in a Sheffield junior league. Mark has his own organisation of scouts and each season he sorts out the best from the dozens of youngsters who he brings for a trial at his wonderful little club.

"Wolves, happy to do so, pay the running expenses of the club and provide the kit and other necessities. Every penny is well spent, for Wath is almost a football gold-mine."

Other players who started under Mark at Wath include Ron Flowers (500-plus League games and 49 England caps), Roy Swinbourne (107 goals in 211 Wolves games), Peter Knowles (70 goals in 200 professional appearances), Bob Hatton (200-plus goals in more than 600 pro games), Jeff Wealands (400 League games) and Alan Sunderland (100 goals in more than 400 games, including an England cap), while he also recommended Alan Ball, Terry Cooper, Bob Wilson and the Charlton brothers, only for them to be either rejected or lured away by other clubs.

Mark's original team played on a small pitch jammed between the railway line and canal, where the 5ft 3in Leeds-born coach ruled the roost.

Mark presented the Mont to the 1941 winners Manvers Main and had earlier played for West Melton Wesleyans, Darfield and Wombwell during their Montagu Cup campaigns in 1923 and 1924.

Steve Ellor

It took Steve Ellor four attempts to get hold of a Mont winners' medal, despite being one of the area's most prolific scorers.

Still playing well into his 40s, Steve struck more than 300 goals, averaging more than 30 a season with Denaby United and scoring nine in a game twice – against Bawtry Town and South Kirkby Colliery Reserves.

He has also appeared in the colours of Groves Social, Mexborough Main Street, Edlington WMC, Rossington Main, Lord Conyers and Conisbrough Cricket Club's Sunday football side.

Steve's first three Montagu Cup finals were all with Groves but they were the losing side in 2002, 2003 and 2005. A switch to Conyers saw him gain his first success, scoring twice in a 3-0 win over Houghton Main in 2006. He returned to Groves and gained a second Mont honour in 2010 with another two goals in the 2-1 win against Wombwell Main, when he was man of the match.

A trophy-laden career also saw Steve pick up the Rotherham Charity Cup, County Senior League Premier Division and Division One titles, two Doncaster Senior League championships plus the Doncaster FA Cup, Doncaster Senior League Cup, Mexborough Sunday League title, the Bourne & Swann Cup, Mick Riley Cup, Fred Whitehead Cup and the Mexborough Challenge Cup.

Jeff Earnshaw

Jeff Earnshaw scored the most Montagu Cup goals of the 1980s with four goals across three victorious finals.

In 1982 he scored twice for Dearne CMW and then got a goal in each of the 1984 and 1987 finals with Mexborough Main Street.

Brian Hill

Brian Hill played in the hugely successful Mexborough Schofield Tech Old Boys team in the 1950s.

For each match, he produced immaculate hand-written reports and has played a big part in the Old Boys keeping in touch with each other in recent years.

Despite now living in Bournemouth, he still organises annual reunions of the Old Boys teams and travels up from Dorset to attend them.

Brian Hill, left, with his 1956 haul of trophies and, above, one of his wonderful hand-written match reports

Kenny Hill with the Mont in 1922 and, top right, in 1957. Above right: Kenny with Brian Dutton and Brian Hill

Kenny King

Kenny King played in the hugely successful Mexborough Schofield Tech Old Boys team in the 1950s and was a prolific centre forward.

They were Montagu Cup finalists in 1956 and went one step better the following season when they beat Hickleton Main in the final. Kenny scored in every round that year – two goals in the first round, a hat-trick in the second, a brace in the third round and a pair in the semi-final replay, before netting one more in the final.

Kenny was born in Denaby in 1936 and went to Balby Street Junior School. In 1947, the school team reached the final of the Totty Cup but lost 1-0 to Darfield Council Junior School. Two weeks later they got revenge with Kenny scoring the only goal of the Totty Shield final to overcome the same opponents. The shield was a play-off between the top teams in the Don and Dearne Junior Leagues.

Kenny played for Conisbrough Secondary Modern School in the Don & Dearne Intermediate League and was then a student at Mexborough Schofield Technical School. In the 1951/2 season he played in the team that won the South Yorkshire Technical Schools League Cup. After leaving school, Kenny joined Tech Old Boys in the Mexborough Association u18 League. He made such an impression that he was asked to play for Doncaster Rovers in the Northern Intermediate u18s and Yorkshire Leagues. Teammates included 15 year old Alick Jeffrey from Rawmarsh, who went on to make his Rovers first-team debut in 1954 age 15 and then played for England u23s when he was just 17.

Kenny helped Tech Old Boys win the Mexborough Challenge Cup and Invitation Cup in 1954/5 and also appeared for Doncaster reserves in the Midland League. That team included Northern Ireland international goalkeeper Harry Gregg and defender Charlie Williams. Both went on to become first-teamers with Gregg moving to Manchester United in 1957 and Williams leaving the game to take up a showbiz career.

Kenny had a trial with Aston Villa and in 1955/6 helped Tech Old Boys to four trophies – Mexborough Association League Cup, Mexborough Association Cup, Mexborough Challenge Cup and Invitation Cup. His season tally of 68 goals came in 34 games, including 14 hat-tricks and a double hat-trick.

Montagu Cup glory came the following season with a nail biting extra-time defeat of Hickleton Main, in which Kenny scored the second goal. The team also won the Yorkshire Old Boys Shield, defeating Beverley Old Grammarians 2-1 under floodlights at Doncaster's Belle Vue ground. He was again leading scorer with 35 goals in 34 games, included four hat-tricks. Aston Villa came calling again and Kenny played in their A and reserve teams. The 1957/8 season saw Kenny at Denaby Tom Hill Old Boys in the Doncaster Senior League but he also turned out for Tech Old Boys in the West Riding Old Boys League. After striking another 35 goals in a season-and a-half with Tech Old Boys in the Sheffield Hatchard League, he moved to Denaby United in the Midland and Central Alliance Leagues. A move to Mexborough Town followed in 1963 in the Yorkshire League before he joined Worksop Town in the Midland League, helping them to the title in 1966. He later joined Skegness Town in the same league.

(Career information courtesy of Brian Hill)

Harry Newey

Harry Newey was a Montagu Cup winner four times with the same team – Manvers Main in 1940, 1941, 1942 and 1945.

He also scored four goals in 12 matches for Bradford City during the final, 1945/6, Wartime Football League season.

Albert Pape

Albert Pape would have played some of his early football in the Montagu Cup but the Elsecar-born player went on to enjoy a long career, lasting from 1914 to 1934.

After leaving Wath Athletic, his stops included Yorkshire Light Infantry, Bolton United, Rotherham County, Notts County, Clapton Orient, Manchester United, Fulham, Rhyl Athletic, Hurst, Darwen, Manchester Central, Hartlepools United, Halifax Town, Burscough Rangers, Horwich RMI and Nelson.

It was his bizarre transfer from Orient to Manchester United that raised eyebrows in 1925.

Orient travelled to face an Old Trafford side that had just sold its star striker. United manager John Chapman telephoned his Orient counterpart Peter Proudfoot before they left London and the two agreed a fee of £1,070 for Albert. They met up at Manchester Piccadilly station just after noon, and Albert quickly agreed terms.

Details were wired to The Football Association and The Football League at about 1.30pm and, although Pape had been named in Orient's starting line-up, he was confirmed as a United player an hour before kick-off. Albert not only started the match in United colours but also scored the third goal in their 4-2 win over his morning employers, as well as hitting a post with a header.

Harry Newey, circled, in the 1942 Manvers Main Mont-winning team

Wilf Race

Wilf Race has been a massive name in Montagu Cup history, both as a player and manager.

He left his post as Maltby chairman just at the right time to help with the cup's 125th anniversary celebrations but is now back in the chair of the Northern Counties East League side.

Wilf won the Montagu Cup three times as a player and four times as a manager.

Onfield success came in 1983, 1984 and 1987 with Mexborough Main Street, while as manager he won the Mont three times on the bounce in 1995, 1996 and 1997 with Denaby & Cadeby Miners Welfare, before raising the cup for a seventh time in 2006 with Conyers.

He came close to another success in 1993 as Goldthorpe Colliery manager but they lost the final in a replay to Brodsworth Miners Welfare.

Pete Pettit

Even before the Montagu Hospital existed, the Pettit family had their shoe business in Mexborough. The business began when Peter Pettit's great-grandfather William Squirrel Pettit bought the shop in Mexborough High Street.

Pete played in the Yorkshire League for Denaby United and Mexborough Town, winning the Montagu Cup on each of the three occasions that he reached a final. He scored in two of those finals.

In 1972 Pete scored the winner for Denaby United in the Yorkshire League Cup final at Belle Vue, Doncaster, against Barton Town.

Pete Pettit heads for goal in a Montagu Cup quarter-final

George and Ted Robledo

The Montagu Cup winner who went on to reach the greatest heights was George Robledo. George and his brothers moved from Chile to West Melton as toddlers and his football talent shone through at Brampton Ellis school.

Ahead of his Mont glory, George scored four goals in each of the Totty Cup finals he played in (1939 and 1940) – a competition for school teams. During four years at the school, he scored 129 times.

In 1944 George guested for Wath Wanderers in the replayed Montagu Cup final. After a brief spell as an amateur with Huddersfield Town, to supplement his income from working down the pit, he signed for Barnsley, moving on to First Division giants Newcastle United, who paid £23,000 for him, plus an extra £3,500 for his brother Ted.

George obviously got a taste for silverware because, within eight years of his Mont success, he had picked up FA Cup medals and appeared in the 1950 World Cup finals for his native Chile.

George played in both the 1951 and 1952 FA Cup finals victories for Newcastle, scoring the winner in 1952 in a team that included Ted. That moment was sketched by 11-year-old John Lennon with the artwork later used on his 1970 album Walls & Bridges.

George was the first overseas player to score the most top-flight league goals – 33 in the 1951/52 season. No overseas player has ever matched that total – Cristiano Ronaldo (31 in 2007/8), Luis Suárez (31, 2013/4) and Mo Salah (32 in 2017/8) have come closest so far. His total of 82 League goals for Newcastle was a record for an overseas player in the top-flight for 46 years, eventually broken in 1999 by Dwight Yorke.

George was also an innovator, bringing lightweight boots to England. In the early 1950s he introduced the new footwear to his team mates after returning from an international match.

George played for Chile 31 times, including each of their matches at the 1950 World Cup. He opened the scoring in a 5-2 victory against USA, a team that had beaten England three days earlier. The Newcastle star was the only player among the 286 from 13 nations who was with a club from outside his own country. He also became the first Football League player from outside the British Isles to play an official game against England.

George Robledo's daughter Elizabeth with a display dedicated to her father and uncle at St James' Park, Newcastle

> 'Robledo was the first overseas player to win the Golden Boot for scoring the most top-flight league goals – 33. No overseas player has ever matched that total'

George and Ted were the first South Americans to play professional football in Britain and, until the appearance of Ricky Villa and Ossie Ardiles for Tottenham in 1981, the only Latin Americans to have played in the FA Cup final.

The brothers were together at Barnsley and both moved to Newcastle United in 1949. While George grabbed the headlines with his goal scoring, alongside 'Wor' Jackie Milburn, Ted was a left-sided defender. He also played for the national team and was part of their 1955

Beatle John Lennon's interpretation of George Robledo's FA Cup final goal

Mum Elsie with George and Ted Robledo

South American Championship squad. The brothers appeared together in the side beaten 1-0 by Argentina in the final in front of 65,000 spectators in Santiago.

After signing for Colo-Colo in their native Chile for £25,000, George's scoring exploits continued as he twice finished as the league's top scorer and his 84 goals in 153 games helped the team to clinch the 1953 and 1956 title.

Although he did not play for England, he was part of the Three Lions' 1962 World Cup squad in Chile, working as an attaché for manager Walter Winterbottom.

While George's career finished in Chile, playing for O'Higgins FC, Ted returned to England and appeared briefly for Notts County.

George died of a heart attack in 1989, while Ted went missing, presumed drowned in 1970.

In a feature for The Athletic sports website by Chris Waugh in 2019, the Robledos' younger brother, Walter, told the story of their lives.

He revealed that none of the brothers could speak Spanish until later in life, creating problems when his siblings were on international duty with Chile, speaking in their broad Yorkshire accents.

"He had to learn some Spanish pretty quickly. I think 'shoot' was the main word he learned!" Walter told The Athletic.

The brothers' mother, Yorkshirewoman Elsie Oliver, travelled to South America to work as a governess. She met and married Aristides Robledo and their three sons were all born in Chile before, in 1932, Elsie returned to England.

George was five, Ted three and Walter just six weeks old when they arrived in England.

"West Melton is where we grew up. It was very enjoyable growing up there, if a little rough," Walter told The Athletic.

As Chris Waugh reported of the Robledos' subsequent fame on Tyneside:

> "George's first goal came against local rivals Sunderland but it was not until the summer of 1949 that he really embedded himself into the side. While in Canada and the United States on a pre-season tour, he wrote articles for the Barnsley Chronicle – detailing trips to Broadway to see the Andrews Sisters and of visiting the former heavyweight champion Jack Dempsey's bar – but, more importantly, he developed a close bond with his teammates.

George and Ted Robledo in their national team shirts

> "None more so than with Milburn. The duo became one of the most feared forward lines in the country, scoring almost 180 goals between them during their four-and-a-half-year partnership."

During his career, George played in every position bar centre-back. At Old Trafford in 1951, he scored a goal before replacing the injured Newcastle goalkeeper.

His 91 goals in 166 games for the Toon came with a scoring ratio of 0.55 – better than that of Alan Shearer, Malcolm Macdonald and Milburn himself.

> **'None of the brothers could speak Spanish, creating problems when his siblings were on international duty with Chile, speaking in their broad Yorkshire accents'**

"Ted played in a less glamorous position to George," Walter told The Athletic. "He was a reliable player, but it was George who scored all the goals."

George's daughter Elizabeth said her dad had told her that he had been approached to play for England but was not eligible because he had never given up his Chilean citizenship.

Two blue plaques were unveiled on the Robledos' former home in the spring of 2022 to commemorate the brothers from Chile who became record breakers in England.

Elizabeth unveiled the plaques after flying from South America, accompanied by Chilean ambassador Francisco Tello.

She was guest of honour at the Montagu Cup final, Barnsley v Peterborough United, Newcastle United v Liverpool and the FA Cup final at Wembley. The FA were marking 150 years of the FA Cup and chose Elizabeth to represent the 1950s.

She was interviewed on BBC's The One Show and was presented with a shirt on the Wembley pitch at half-time in the FA Cup final. She had to fund her trip by auctioning her father's memorabilia. The 1952 FA Cup final shirt sold for £7,500.

Tony Rodgers (circled) with his Ford United teammates after their 1960 Mont victory over Houghton Main

Tony Rodgers

Tony Rodgers played in two consecutive Montagu Cup finals for Ford United, in 1960 and 1961.

However, the contrast between them could not have been greater. There was joy in the first one, thanks to a 4-0 win over Houghton Main but heartache 12 months later when Tony suffered a broken leg during a 4-3 defeat against Parkgate Welfare. He ended the match being treated in the Montagu Hospital.

The Ford Motor Company had a factory in Doncaster at the time and Ford United were the works' football team.

Tony played in the reserve teams of Doncaster Rovers and Charlton Athletic and was also with Denaby United. While serving in the RAF, he was a triple jump champion.

Tony's son, Chris, was a mascot for both the Mont finals and the pair went on to play together for Boston United in the Northern Premier League.

Mascot Chris Rodgers shakes hands with the Houghton captain ahead of Ford's 1960 win

Tony Rodgers, left, and his son Chris, right, before the 1961 Montagu Cup final

Arthur Roberts collects the Montagu Cup for the victorious Conisbrough Northcliffe side in 1937 while, right, he presents the trophy to Swinton Athletic's 1986 winning captain Geoff Cooke

Arthur Roberts

Arthur Roberts captained Conisbrough Northcliffe to Montagu Cup victory in 1937, while almost half a century later he presented the magnificent trophy to 1986 winners Swinton Athletic.

His daughter, Norah Dadswell, said: "I don't think he was on the Mont committee but he presented many trophies and never missed a Montagu Cup final. Football was his life until he died at 89 years old."

Lionel Smith

Lionel Smith played in the 1939 Montagu Cup final for Yorkshire Tar Distillers. Four months later he joined Arsenal and played 155 times for them, despite having to wait almost nine years to make his debut due to World War Two. He was capped six times by England.

Jimmy Sansome

Dalton-born Jimmy Sansome played for Silverwood in their 1954 Montagu Cup victory over Ings Lane.

However, it is in another sport he is better known. Incredibly, Sansome has beaten five world snooker champions and also narrowly lost to Joe Johnson (on a black ball) the year before he won the world title.

Jimmy's heyday came in the decade before money came into snooker, otherwise he would have been a household name.

Jimmy beat Fred Davis, John Pullman, Ray Reardon and John Spencer. He had been only 15 years old when he beat John Donaldson.

The day after the Montagu Cup final, Jimmy and his Silverwood team mates had to play in the Rotherham Charity Cup final but a fatigued side lost to New Stubbin at Millmoor.

A couple of years before this, Jimmy had represented the British Armed Forces at the Olympic Stadium, Berlin. He was the only player not assigned to a Football League club. Sheffield United wanted to sign him but his real passion was snooker.

A Rotherham Advertiser feature on Jimmy Sansome, above, and, left, with snooker trophies then and now

Rex Trickett and his wife Edna are interviewed by ITV Calendar's Jon Hill in 2022. Far left, with his Mont trophy from 1958 and, inset alongside George 'Shudda' Mitchell, who is holding the cup

Rex Trickett

1958 Mont winner Rex Trickett, who was 92 in 2022, was, along with his twin brothers George and Harold, on Manchester City's books.

Rex played a few reserve matches for them before National Service took him to Africa and the Middle East.

On his return, Rex played local football for Swinton Bowbroom WMC, where he enjoyed a lot of success, notably when they won the Montagu Cup.

Rex also played for Swinton Athletic and Denaby United and remembers getting paid half-a-crown by Denaby for playing against a Sheffield Wednesday team.

The inside-right scored two goals in an Army Cadet final at Bramall Lane.

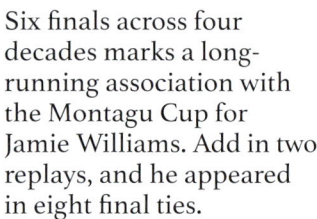

Jamie Williams

Six finals across four decades marks a long-running association with the Montagu Cup for Jamie Williams. Add in two replays, and he appeared in eight final ties.

He started in 1998 with a victory for Wombwell Main over Mexborough Main Street. A replay defeat to Dearne CMW followed in the colours of Westville in 2004 before a success back with Wombwell Main in 2007. Wombwell won again the following year but Jamie was with beaten finalists Westville. Revenge was gained in 2018 when Westville beat Wombwell but Jamie suffered defeat to Swinton with Westville in 2020.

The record breakers...

The most recorded Montagu Cup final appearances is seven. This feat has been achieved by Rob Branagan, Ian Cotton, Jon Billups, Shawn Mitchell and Jake Simon.

Shawn Mitchell was awarded the man of the match award in his last three finals.

Terry Simon has been involved in 10 finals – three as a player and seven as a manager.

Wilf Race has also been involved in seven finals, three as a player and four as a manager.

The player with most Montagu Cup winners' medals is Dean Oxer, who won all six of the finals that he played in.

Paul 'Tupper' Cooke played in six Montagu Cup finals and was on the winning side on four occasions. He was captain of Denaby & Cadeby Miners Welfare when they won the Mont for three consecutive seasons in the mid-1990s.

Jamie Williams also played in six finals for Westville WMC and Wombwell Main.

There may be others, as the reporting of the Montagu Cup players in the early days was often restricted to surnames.

Shawn Mitchell, Terry Simon and Dean Oxer

The elite...

These are some of the players who appeared in the Montagu Cup and, according to the English National Football Archive, played at an elite level. Years in brackets indicates a year they played in a Montagu Cup match.

Wally Ardron (1944): Rotherham United, Nottingham Forest
Tommy Astill (1913): Leeds City
Jack Aston (1905): Walsall, Arsenal, Small Heath, Doncaster Rovers
Percy Beaumont (1918): Sheffield United, Barnsley, Southend United
Troy Bennett (2007): Scarborough
Charles Bembridge (1930): Rotherham United
Joe Beresford (1924): Aston Villa, Preston North End, Swansea, England and FA Cup final
Kenny Boden (1970): Doncaster Rovers, Newcastle KB United, Sydney City, Sydney Croatia and Australia

Joe Beresford, b1906, played in the 1924 Montagu Cup final before making 224 appearances for Aston Villa. He earned one cap for England, on May 16, 1934, against Czechoslovakia. Joe was in Preston North End's beaten FA Cup final side of 1937.

Philip Bratley (1904): Doncaster Rovers, Barnsley, Liverpool, Rotherham (Town and County) and FA Cup winner
Jimmy Broadhead (1919): Nelson
Wilf Brown (1942): New Brighton, Rotherham United
Jack Burkinshaw (1907): Grimsby Town, The Wednesday, Bradford (Park Avenue)
Stan Burton (1940): Doncaster Rovers, Wolves, West Ham United and FA Cup final
Fred Bye (1906): Football League and international referee
Frank Chivers (1930): Barnsley, Huddersfield Town, Blackburn Rovers
John Cocker (1942): England Schoolboys
Wilf Copping (1929): Leeds United, Arsenal, England and FA Cup and Football League title winner
Christopher Crapper (1905): The Wednesday, Grimsby Town
Sid Dawson (1914): Grimsby Town, Northampton Town
Ray Dixon (1950): Rotherham United
George Dobson (1919): Barnsley, Norwich City, Rotherham County

Ernest Dowson (1901): Doncaster Rovers
James Arthur Dyer (1910): Barnsley, Manchester United
Jack Edwards (1942): Rotherham United
Alfred William Francis (1908): Barnsley
Cyril Grant (1940): Arsenal, Fulham, Southend United
Harry Gray (1940): Barnsley, Bournemouth, Southend United
Tommy Hakin (1905): Grimsby Town
Jim Hancock (1902): Chesterfield
Cyril Hannaby (1944): Hull City, Halifax Town
Ezra Holmes (1906): Gainsborough Trinity, Birmingham
Jack Hubbard (1945): Notts County, Scunthorpe & Lindsey United
Peter Kitchen (late 60s): Doncaster Rovers, Orient, Fulham, Cardiff City
Walter Langton (1901): Doncaster Rovers
William Lawley (1902): Barnsley

Wilf Copping, b1909, played in the Mont quarter-final of 1929 for Middlecliffe against eventual runners-up Conisbrough Welfare.
He joined Leeds United later that year, playing more than 160 times, before going to Arsenal in 1934. The Football League named Wilf as one of their 100 Legends as part of their centenary celebrations and the 'Iron Man' won two Football League titles, the FA Cup and two Charity Shields.

Philip Bratley, b1880, played more than 150 games as a centre half, right back and left half and won the FA Cup with Barnsley in 1912. He started his career with Doncaster Rovers but played only three games before going on to play for both Rotherham teams, County and Town. He scored for Town in their 1904 defeat by Mexborough Town. Philip moved to Liverpool and ended his career with Worksop Town.

Edward Layton, b1883, was a Football League champion with Aston Villa in 1909/10. He had earlier played for South Kirkby in the 1906 Montagu Cup final, having joined them from Sheffield United. He went on to play for Middlesbrough before moving to Australia for two years. Although a full back, he played an 'international' between New South Wales and Queensland as centre forward and got the winner. Edward later turned out for Whitby Town, Cardiff City and Stockport County.

Billy Linward, b1880, started his career with Grimsby All Saints before joining Doncaster Rovers in 1895. The outside left won the Mont with them in 1901 and went on to a long career with West Ham United, Woolwich Arsenal and Norwich City, before a spell with Kilmarnock and a period of non-League football at Maidstone United and Dartford.

Edward Layton (1906): Aston Villa, Middlesbrough, Cardiff City and FL title winner
Manny Lindley (1901): Doncaster Rovers
Billy Linward (1901): Doncaster Rovers, West Ham United, Woolwich Arsenal
Harry Maycock (1921): Southend United
Matt Moralee (1942): Grimsby Town, Aston Villa, Leicester City
Kenneth Parkinson (1945): Lincoln City
Francis Pepper (1898): Newton Heath, Barnsley, Doncaster Rovers
Mick Prendergast (1983): Sheffield Wednesday, Barnsley
Frank Rayner (1942): Mansfield Town, Burnley, Notts Co
Norman Rimmington (1955): Barnsley, Hartlepools United
Willis Rippon (1907): Bristol City, Woolwich Arsenal, Grimsby Town and FA Cup semis
George Robledo (1944): Huddersfield Town, Barnsley, Newcastle Utd, Chile, FA Cup winner
Harry Rothery (1903): Sheffield United, Nottm Forest
Jack Selkirk (1960): Rotherham United
Alf Smelt (1919): Leeds United
Jack Smelt (1919): Portsmouth, The Wednesday
Joe Smith (1912): Birmingham, Chesterfield
Lionel Smith (1939): Arsenal, Watford, England, FA Cup and Football League title winner
Ernie Surtees (1907): Barnsley
Tommy Thorpe (1903): Doncaster Rovers, Barnsley, Northampton Town
Tommy Tompkins (1903): Doncaster Rovers, Leeds City
Willis Walker (1913): Leeds City, South Shields, Bradford (Park Avenue)
Billy Whitehurst (1979): Hull City, Newcastle Utd, Oxford Utd, Reading, Sunderland, Sheffield Utd, Stoke City, Doncaster Rovers, Crewe
Tony Wilcox (1962): Barnsley

> Clifford Willock won the 1927 Montagu Cup with Goldthorpe. Tragically, four years later he was one of 45 fatalities at the Bentley Colliery after a gas explosion.

Frank Rayner, b1913, was on the books of Charlton, Barnsley and Rotherham United without making an appearance but got his chance at Mansfield Town, where he netted eight times in 17 games before a move to Burnley, where he added another seven in 79. Frank finished his professional career with Notts County before appearing in the 1942 Mont final.

Willis Rippon, b 1886, made a name for himself north of the border after a 1907 Montagu Cup win with Kilnhurst Town. The centre forward had played for Hackenthorpe, Rawmarsh Albion and Sandhill Rovers before being 'discovered' by Bristol City, where he scored 13 times in 36 games. Willis also hit 41 goals in 56 games for Arsenal, Brentford and Grimsby but was just as prolific with Hamilton Academical, where he got 22 goals in 39 games.

Clubs

Some of the sides who have created their own piece of Montagu Cup history

Ian Smith wheels away after netting Denaby & Cadeby's equaliser in the 1988 final

Denaby & Cadeby Miners Welfare

Formed in 1980, Denaby & Cadeby made a swift impact on the Montagu Cup honours board.

They won it in 1988 and by 1997 had chalked up a five-out-of-five winning record, including three on the bounce in the mid-90s.

1988: 2-1 v Swinton Athletic
1991: 2-1 v Swinton Athletic
1995: 2-0 v Mexborough Main Street
1996: 4-2 v Wath Saracens
1997: 2-1 v Wath Saracens

Wilf Race managed the team, with Paul Cooke as his captain, for their hat-trick. They also had a superb record in other competitions, winning three consecutive divisional titles in the Sheffield County Senior – Division Three 1986/7, Division Two 1987/8 and Division One 1988/9, before coming second in the Premier Division on 1990/1.

They also won the Fullerton Cup in 1987/8 and 1989/90, as well as the Mexborough Challenge Cup in 1988/9, having been runners-up in 1986/7.

The club became Denaby United Reserves in 1997 and continued until about 2002, according to Steve Watkin, who supplied the information.

Denaby & Cadeby Miners Welfare after their first win in 1988

Another Mont was added in 1991 before the first of a hat-trick in 1995

Victories in 1996 and 1997 completed a treble for Denaby & Cadeby

Denaby United

Denaby United are arguably the most famous of the area's non-League clubs.

Formed in 1895, United reached the first round of the FA Cup three times and enjoyed a record crowd of 5,200 for the visit of Southport in 1927.

Their players included future England internationals Sam Cowan and Jack Barker, while former England player Mel Sterland also played for them.

Among the Midland League club's honours were six Montagu Cups, appearing in 12 finals.

1902: Beat Newhill 3-0
1915: Beat Mexborough GCL 2-0 (2-2)
1919: Lost to Kimberworth OB 1-2
1944: Lost to Wath Wdrs 1-2 (3-3)
1955: Beat Bowbroom WMC 2-0
1958: Lost to Bowbroom WMC 0-2
1967: Lost to High Terrace 0-1
1970: Beat Northcliffe 1-0 (0-0)
1974: Beat Jungle United 2-1 (1-1)
1978: Beat Houghton Main 4-2
1999: Lost to Mexborough MS 0-1
2000: Lost to Mexborough MS 0-1

Denaby ceased activity in 2002 after a dispute over the use of their Tickhill Square ground.

A new, unrelated, United was formed in 2011 and now compete for village honours with Denaby Main, who moved into the famous old ground.

Three or more

The following clubs have won the Mont more than any other...
- 8 – Swinton Athletic
- 7 – Wombwell Main
- 7 – Mexborough Main St
- 6 – Denaby United
- 5 – Denaby & Cadeby MW
- 4 – Manvers Main
- 4 – Parkgate Welfare
- 4 – AFP
- 4 – Rawmarsh Welfare
- 4 – Hickleton Main
- 4 – Houghton Main
- 3 – Goldthorpe United
- 3 – Mexborough Town

Denaby United 1914/15 winners – Standing at rear, from left: W Marshall (captain), W Rotherham, C Blaby.
Back row: J Heslop (committee), J E Wheellcor (committee), H Fitton, R Purdy, P Hall, O Bransby, L Moseley, T Dabbs, J Ingledowe (committee), H Gomersall (committee).
Front row: MT Thompson (Montagu Hospital secretary), J Widdison, P Jepson, HW Smith (president), GH Jackson, J Madin, JT Clayton (secretary). The children at the front are not identified

Denaby United's 1969/70 squad – Back row: Jimmy Wiggles, Steve Toyne, Kenny Whitehead, Pete Pettit, Des Harvey, Pete Whitehead.
Front: Dick Sumpner, Roger Willey, Howard Morley, Harold Sapey (player-manager), Richard England, Neil Gray

Player-manager Harold Sapey with the Montagu Cup following Denaby United's 1970 success. Immediately to the right is Harry Lawrence (president) with Jim Reeve (chairman) and Tom Sapey (secretary), extreme right

Hampden Road's pavilion, main picture. Inset: Tom Dennett, Mexborough & Wath Hospitals' Comforts Fund chairman, presents the Montagu Cup to Mexborough Town captain Brian Tonks in 1977. 'Town' teams also won in 1904 and 1905

Mexborough Athletic

The Hampden Road base of Mexborough Athletic has been home of the Mont since the very beginning.

Although several incarnations of clubs have called Hampden Road their ground, none have stood the test of time.

The current Mexborough Athletic FC was founded by Steve Poole and Linda Carlton in 2012.

Prior to that, the sports grounds were leased to various football clubs and were home to Mexborough Cricket Club.

The grounds were looked after by Hughie Tingle, a member of the cricket club, and by Doncaster Metropolitan Borough Council, who ensured the grounds were kept in excellent condition for many years.

Mexborough Athletic are the present tenants, consisting of a men's Sunday side, an open-age ladies' team, under-16 girls' teams and under-14 and under-9s boys' teams.

The football pitches and grounds are maintained by Steve Poole and the borough council and are all run and maintained by volunteers.

Among the 'Mexborough' teams to have won

Linda Carlton and Steve Poole with the Montagu Cup

the Mont are versions of Town (1899, 1904, 05 and 77) plus Rovers (1918), Athletic (1934) as well as Main Street (1983, 84, 87, 99, 2000, 05 and 08 – see opposite) and Schofield Tech Old Boys (1957).

The main stand at Mexborough Athletic's Hampden Road ground

Different kits, same club. Mexborough Main Street after their four Mont wins

Manvers Main

During the war years, professional players from the Football League had more freedom to play for local teams than at any other time.

Manvers Main benefitted more than most from this influx of talent with the pit offering much employment.

According to one report, Manvers fielded five Division One players in a Montagu Cup third-round tie in 1940. They won that year's final with a record-breaking 8-0 scoreline, with Stan Burton, of Wolves, and Arsenal's Lionel Smith in the line-up.

Manvers had tighter matches in their Mont wins in 1941 and 1942 before another war-time victory in 1945. Albert Horner played in all three of the consecutive final victories.

Stan Burton, above, Lionel Smith, above right, and Albert Horner, right, were all key members of the Manvers Main team in the early years of World War Two

Mexborough Main Street

Flying the flag for Mexborough – an excerpt from the Sheffield Star of Wednesday, October 5, 2005:

Mexborough Main Street were formed by disgruntled players who were being 'rested' in High Terrace's reserve side. They went to the committee of the Main Street Club in Mexborough, persuaded them to offer their backing, and so began a relationship that lasted over 40 years.

Ian Cotton, Pete Cutts and Brian Wray, with the help of Cyril Drabble, founded Mexborough Main Street.

"Ian, Pete and Brian were in the second team at High Terrace and wanted to break away and form their own team," said Cyril. "I offered to help them set up and as we were all members of the Main Street Club anyway, they were the natural choice for us to see about forming a team. They were more than happy to and even bought us a kit.

"We joined the Doncaster Senior League, played our games at the back of the Plant Hotel and started in the autumn of 1965."

The club progressed to the County Senior League in the early 1980s, by which time they had eloped to the LNER ground in Swinton.

The move to Mexborough Athletic Club was made a few years later, by which time they had lifted the County Senior League title for the first time in 1987, a feat they were to repeat in 1994.

The trophies didn't stop in 1994, with Main Street winning the Montagu Cup and Rotherham Charity Cup in the same year in both 2000 and in 2005.

Swinton Athletic

Swinton Athletic have won the Montagu Cup more than any other club – eight times – and have also been beaten in five finals.

Remarkably, their first five final appearances were in consecutive leap years – winners in 1964, 1968, 1972 and 1980, losing in 1976.

They were also winners in 1986, 1989, 2020 and 2021 and beaten in the finals of 1988, 1991, 2014 and 2015.

Athletic were founded in 1946 but folded in 2005 when they changed name to Dearne/Swinton and then Dearne Colliery.

They were reformed in 2008 as Swinton Station Athletic by two former Athletic players, Andrew Billups and Martin Rouane, based at the Station Hotel. By 2012, the club was back as Swinton Athletic and, as well as Mont finals has enjoyed league success too.

1964 winning captain Brian Hyde with the cup and the club committee

Andy Mangham scores Swinton's goal in their 1991 final defeat

Six of Swinton Athletic's Montagu Cup-winning line-ups

Wombwell Main with the 2009 Mont, the last time they lifted the trophy. They have since reached three more finals

Wombwell Main

Wombwell Main have won the Montagu Cup seven times – 1906, 1998, 2001-03, 2007 and 2009.

Wombwell Main Cricket & Sports Association started about 1856, with the football team playing its first match in September 1880. There are only four football clubs in South Yorkshire that are older (Sheffield, Hallam, Sheffield Wednesday and Doncaster Rovers).

The 1905/06 season was particularly successful for the club. They won the Montagu Cup, the Rotherham Charity Cup and the Barnsley Beckett Cup – a feat no other club has achieved. They also played in the FA Cup but with little success.

Wombwell's three consecutive Montagu Cup wins at the turn of the 21st century is a feat only matched by Hickleton Main (1911-13), Manvers Main (1940-42), Rawmarsh Welfare (1949-51), Denaby & Cadeby Miners Welfare (1995-97) and AFP (2012-14)

After seven successful final appearances, Wombwell have lost in their last three – 2010, 2018 and 2019.

AFP

Rotherham Sunday League team, AFP, had never entered the Montagu Cup until they rattled off a quickfire triple from 2012 to 2014, beating Swinton teams in every final.

The Kimberworth Park-based team won a fourth Mont in 2016.

This was a proud era for their secretary Malcolm Gabbitas, who passed away recently.

Reece Wesley was captain for each of the four victories.

Debut glory for AFP, who won the Mont at the first time of asking in 2012

Rawmarsh Welfare

Rawmarsh's first 'win' came in 1949, albeit in unique circumstances. For the only time in Montagu Cup history, the trophy was shared after 1-1 and 0-0 draws against Kilnhurst. See full story, page 39.

The following year, the same two teams contested the final and again a replay and extra time was needed to separate them. This time it did with Les Swales' hat-trick settling things. The triple was sealed with a 2-1 win against Swinton Bowbroom WMC in 1951 – after yet another replay!

Rawmarsh won the Yorkshire League in 1970 and also have two Sheffield & Hallamshire Senior Cups and an FA Cup first round appearance to their name.

They also reached the third round of the FA Amateur Cup, with crowds of up to 6,600.

Rawmarsh Welfare 1949/50

Goldthorpe United

Goldthorpe won the Montagu Cup in 1927, 1930 and 1931.

An earlier Goldthorpe Miners' Institute side had won it in 1909. Goldthorpe United were top dog in town in the 1920s and 30s though, chalking up 22 FA Cup ties between 1928 and 1935, including wins over Maltby Main Colliery, Hatfield Main, Norton Woodseats, Hallam and Yorkshire Amateur, reaching the third qualifying round in 1930/1.

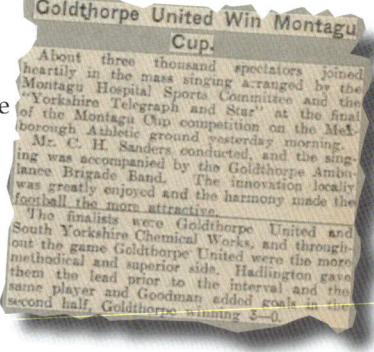

Hickleton Main

Hickleton's 1910 semi-final against Conisbrough Swifts was an epic contest taking six matches to produce a winner (see page 26).

The Swifts won the fourth match, but Hickleton Main successfully appealed. In total, the teams had met 10 times throughout the season.

To make up for lost time, Hickleton were cup winners again in the following two years.

Hickleton's 1911 Montagu Cup-winning line-up

Houghton Main

Houghton were one of many South Yorkshire teams to try their luck in the Yorkshire League during its formative years.

They were members in its second season, 1921/22, when they finished top. However, a year later they were 15th of 16 teams and left.

They were successful in the Doncaster League (winning it seven times, including a title quadruple, 1972-1976) before making their way into the Sheffield & Hallamshire County Senior League where they gained double promotions to the Premier Division between 2002 and 2005 before taking a year out, only to repeat their rapid ascent between 2010 and 2012, this time with the Division Two and One title to their name. Houghton were Montagu Cup winners in 1969, 1975 and 2017.

Houghton Main with an impressive 1974/5 haul

Parkgate Welfare

The history of Parkgate Welfare is little known. They entered the FA Cup in 1950/1 and the FA Amateur Cup in 1952/3. Welfare won the Rotherham Charity Cup in 1948 and 1953 as well as the Sheffield Association League in 1962. Other than that, the record books are blank – apart from their Montagu Cup wins of 1948, 1953, 1961 and 1962.

Parkgate's history is tightly linked to the neighbouring steelworks, which was founded in 1823. Other clubs to carry the name have been Parkgate & Rawmarsh United, Parkgate Works Sports and the present Parkgate FC, who were formed in 1969 and also had BSC and RES suffixes.

Parkgate Welfare won both the Montagu Cup and Rotherham Charity Cup in 1948

Hospital and Comforts Fund

The Montagu Cottage Hospital was opened in 1890

Funds raised during Montagu Cup competitions go to the Montagu Hospital, which was built in 1890 to serve the public of Mexborough and surrounding districts.

An increase in the number of accidents in local industries led to calls for local hospital services towards the end of the 19th century. Anyone who sustained injuries had to be treated in their own home with the more seriously hurt being transported, usually by horse-drawn trap, to infirmaries at Doncaster or Rotherham.

A committee was formed, with discussions taking place whether to buy, build or rent a property that would be suitable for the purpose.

Unexpectedly, the building was provided on a long lease and at a nominal rent by Andrew Montagu and subscriptions to help fund it were donated by local industries, churches and charitable organisations, as well as wealthy local residents.

That meant the Montagu Cottage Hospital was officially opened in January 1890 in Bank Street, Mexborough, with 14 beds.

Over the first six years of its existence, the local population grew, with more than 2,000 houses built, which meant extensions to increase the size of the hospital were required. A football competition was launched to help raise funds towards the hospital's expansion with the first competition run in the 1896/7 season.

It soon became necessary to look for a new location for the hospital to cope with the additional demand placed on its resources. The first proposals were put forward only five years after the hospital had opened and in 1901 trustees of the Montagu family agreed to sell a small piece of land at the corner of Cemetery Road and Adwick Road.

Andrew Montagu was an early, major benefactor

The Montagu Hospital is now part of the Doncaster and Bassetlaw Teaching Hospitals NHS Foundation Trust

Land was obtained at a price of £756 for one-and-a-quarter acres for the new hospital to be built, with the funding coming from the sale of the Cottage Hospital (£2,000), committee funds (£2,000) and Mr FJO Montagu (£1,500).

And so, the Montagu Cottage Hospital became the Montagu Hospital as we know it today.

It is now managed by the Doncaster and Bassetlaw Teaching Hospitals NHS Foundation Trust, which also includes Bassetlaw District General Hospital and Doncaster Royal Infirmary.

However, the Montagu Cup still plays its part in supporting the hospital.

The Hospital Comforts Fund was launched in 1948, upon the establishment of the NHS, and the Montagu Charity Cup committee has raised many thousands of pounds for it.

Funds are spent by the Comforts Fund trustees for the relief of patients who are sick, convalescent, handicapped or infirm; the provision of amenities in the hospital for patients and staff and generally in support of the charitable work of the hospital.

The Montagu Cup has raised tens of thousands of pounds over the last 70 years, including £20,000 in the past 10. This has enabled trustees to provide items not available through the NHS.

As well as the Mont, money for the Comforts Fund comes from the profits of a tea shop run by volunteers and from legacies, as well as donations from individuals and other charitable organisations.

In the last decade money from the Comforts Fund has helped pay for an indoor corridor to be built, which linked the main building to the rehabilitation centre. Previously, this was an outdoor route.

Other expenditure goes towards providing newspapers for patients while, at Christmas, gifts for patients and decorations are provided.

The fund also helped provide a £17,000 freehand robotic camera controller, which provides surgeons with a clear, magnified view of the part of the body they are operating on.

Although the Montagu Cup is associated with football, previously the amount was boosted at a variety of events, including tennis, bowls and a concert.

The 2022 campaign saw a record £5,000 donated by the Montagu Cup to the Comforts Fund.

The 125th anniversary year saw the donation boosted by several innovations, including pin badges and a Meet at the Mont event, while ITV covered the final.

The hard-working Montagu Cup committee care passionately about maintaining the tradition of their competition and raising funds for their local hospital, determined to pass on the legacy of the past 125 years, created by their predecessors.

Montagu Cup committee chairman Ian Walsh, left, with Comforts Fund treasurer Ian Wright and Mick Swann, of main sponsors Stelrad, at the 2022 presentation

These plaques take pride of place on the walls of the Montagu Hospital

Committee

Players and match officials are an integral part of the Montagu Cup on the field but there is an equally essential team hard at work behind the scenes – the committee.

The current committee, as at July 2022, consists of chairman Ian Walsh, secretary Jamie Ball, treasurer Barrie Dalby, Martin Birley and Andrew Wordsworth. Barrie was secretary (2004-2022), while Alan Cliff (1984-2003) and Bernard Hodgkinson have also held that role.

Presidents have included Derrick Jones, Roy Parkin and Gordon Swann with the treasurer's position previously filled by Dennis Townsend and Janet Helliwell among others.

Wilf Polhill, Peter Taylor and George Wordsworth have served as vice-president and previous committee members have included Steve Venables, Sammy South, Peter Walker, Terry Collinson, Kevin Mallin, David Hanby, Gordon Swann, Michael Stocks, Adrian Pender, Hayley Pender, Brian Hardeman, Colin Taylor (Peter's brother), Barney Randall and Mr M South.

Committee members pictured at previous presentations include: Tom Stone, Peter Taylor, Wilf Polhill, George Wordsworth, Derrick Jones, Andrew Wordsworth, Alan Cliff, Brian Hardeman, Roy Parkin and Steve Venables.

Captains

2022: Gaz Mundy
2021: Alex Wilkinson
2020: Owen Fieldsend
2019: Dan Patterson
2018: Jamie Williams
2017: Adam Stead
2016: Reece Wesley
2015: Danny South
2014: Reece Wesley
2013: Reece Wesley
2012: Reece Wesley
2011: Andy Whitehead
2010: Callum Black
2009: Troy Bennett
2008: Mark Nisbett
2007: Troy Bennett
2006: Martin Barnfield
2005: Gareth Petch
2004: Richard Butcher
2003: Pete Smith
2002: Micky Pearce
2001: Wayne Cunningham
2000: Chris France
1999: Chris France
1998: Terry Simon
1997: Paul Cooke
1996: Paul Cooke
1995: Paul Cooke
1994: Alan Watson
1993: Phil Thomas
1992: Phil Thomas
1991: Colin Squires
1990: Joe Maloney
1989: John Hodgson
1988: Kevin Loftus
1987: Jeff Earnshaw
1986: Geoff Cooke
1985: Barry Whitehead
1984: Gary Skidmore
1983: Gary Skidmore
1982: Joe Maloney
1981: Russ Evans
1980: Neil Spencer
1979: Steve Whitehead
1978: Doug Hemmingway
1977: Brian Tonks
1976: John Wheeler
1975: Tom Gregory
1974: Tony Lowe
1973: Dick Bell
1972: Paul Senior
1971: Keith Whitehouse
1970: Harold Sapey
1969: Derek Rawson
1968: Brian Hyde
1967: Terry Collinson
1966: Terry Collinson
1964: Brian Hyde
1963: Benny Slade
1962: Walt Taylor
1961: Walt Taylor
1960: Roy Shepherd
1959: Dennis Ager
1958: George 'Shudda' Mitchell
1957: Don Lancashire
1955: John Roberts
1954: Jimmy Egan
1953: Doug Page
1945: Raynor
1942: Matt Moralee
1941: W Deakin
1937: Arthur Roberts
1933: Sid Mace
1932: Frank Sylvester
1931: Jim Hadlington
1929: George Walker
1928: Hill
1927: Jim Hadlington
1925: Chapman
1923: John Gladwin
1922: Jimmy Ludlam
1919: J Harrison
1918: Percy Beaumont
1915: W Marshall
1914: Len Harvey
1911: Jack Eades
1906: Turton
1905: Billy Biggs
1902: Lawley
1901: Jagger Holling
1897: Arthur James Allen

Denaby & Cadeby captain Colin Squires receives the Mont from Dennis Priestley in 1991

Houghton Main captain Adam Stead with the 2017 Montagu Cup

Swinton Athletic's Alex Wilkinson with the Mont in 2021

    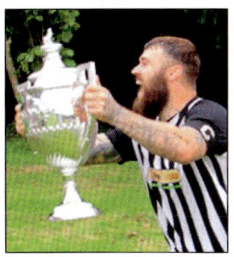 

John Wheeler, Rawmarsh, 1976 | *Phil Thomas, Brodsworth, '93* | *Wath St James' Alan Watson, '94* | *Danny South, of Memories, 2015* | *Owen Fieldsend, of Swinton, '20* | *Scawthorpe's Gaz Mundy '22*

Referees
The men in the middle

Mick Cooke refereed the 2022 final with his team of Paul Ardron, Chris Hargrave and Steve Taylor, pictured with Gaz Mundy and Tommy Needham, the captains of Scawthorpe Athletic and Dog Daisy United respectively

We all have a moan about them at times, some of us more vociferously than others, but, without their presence, there would have been no Mont finals – or any games for that matter!

Here are the men who have played their usually unheralded part in Mont final history:

2022: Referee – Mick Cooke (Assistants – linesmen/fourth official): Paul Ardron, Chris Hargrave, Steve Taylor

2021: Chris Cooper (above)
Ian Walsh, Matthew Bacon, David Hobson

2021 referee Chris Cooper

Mick Poole was the referee for the 2020 Montagu Cup final

2020: Mick Poole
Malcolm Levitt, Roger Webb, John Nicolson

2019: Dave Hobson
Mick Poole, Scott Atkinson, Mick Cooke

2018: Roger Webb
John Nicolson, Paul Ardron, Pete Bailey

2017: Steve Grainger
Mick Poole, Lee Bramley, Paul Jackson

2016: Ian Walsh
Pete Bailey, Paul Ardron, Lee Bramley

2015: Kevin Nelthorpe
Steve Grainger, Ian Walsh, Roger Webb

2014: Pete Bailey
Paul Emmett, Kevin Nelthorpe, Steve Grainger

2013: Colin Parker
Matt Bacon, Paul Humphries, Kevin Nelthorpe

The man in the middle for the 2019 final was Dave Hobson

Steve Grainger was the 2017 referee

Ian Walsh was the referee for the 2016 Mont final

2012: John Nicolson
　Terry Whitehead, Paul Ardron, Pete Bailey

2011: Ian Dring
　Colin Parker, Mick Poole, Matt Bacon

2010: Matt Bacon
　Steve Venables, Ian Dring, Paul Froggatt

2009: Brian Hyde
　Pete Bailey, Matt Bacon, Paul Ardron

2008: Brian Hardeman
　Paul Rouane, Chris Cooper, Colin Parker

2007: Paul Ardron
　Terry Whitehead, Paul Emmett, Des Nutting

2006: Steve Taylor
　David Catling, Paul Ardron, Paul Emmett

2005: Martin Birley
　Colin Parker, Steve Taylor, Brian Elwell

2004: Mick Poole
　David Hobson, Pete Bailey, Steve Taylor

2003: Paul Rouane
　Gordon Swann, Brian Hyde, Chris Cooper

2002: Terry Whitehead

2001: Chris Cooper

2000: David Catling

1999: Phil Oxley

1998: Dave Hobson

Making history – the two referees who have won the Mont

The only two people to have both played and refereed in Montagu Cup finals are Brian 'Boe' Hyde and Gordon Swann.

Brian played for Swinton Athletic in the victorious finals of 1964 (as captain) and 1968. Gordon was part of Northcliffe's 1971 winning team.

In 1987 Brian refereed the final between Mexborough Main Street and BSC Parkgate, while Gordon was running the line.

Gordon was in charge in 1990, while Brian was referee for a rare second occasion in 2009. They both ran the line in the 2003 final.

For several decades, the pair also volunteered to officiate in the Totty Cup final for local primary schools.

Brian 'Boe' Hyde and Gordon Swann have won the Mont as players and also refereed the final

Brian receives the 1964 Mont and, right, most of the Northcliffe team in 1971 – Gordon was missing!

The 2010 Montagu Cup final was refereed by Matt Bacon

1997: Gary Mellor
1996: Peter Bailey
1995: Colin Parker
1994: Eric Fieldsend
1993: Steve Wordsworth
1992: Steve Cooke
1991: Steve Venables
1990: Gordon Swann
   Eric Fieldsend,
   Steve Wordsworth
1989: Terry Whittaker
1988: Cyril Coles
1987: Brian Hyde
   Colin Beasley, Gordon Swann
1986: Alec Clyde
1985: Neil Hemmingway
1984: Cyril Coles
   Richard Russell, Pat Gallagher
1983: Brian Hardeman
1982: Not known

1981: Barry Dickinson
1980: Melvyn Caddick
1978: John Norton
1977: Brian Fletcher
1976: Alan Martin
1975: Terry Ashford
1972: John Sheldon
1971: Tom Richardson
   Dennis Simms
1970: George Wordsworth
   D Jones, T Richardson
1969: Derrick Jones
1968: George Flint
1967: John Jeffcote
1966: D Belk
1964: Matt Taylor
1963: Bob Raby
1962: B Lumb
1961: JW Price
1960: J Smith
1956: Sid Jackson
1951: Colin Taylor
1946: Walter Scattergood
1945: Herbert Clarke
1944: Lol Wesson
1936: J Humphries
1935: Douglas Bisby
   E Butler, C Hague
1932: Lol Wesson
1931: T Swinburne
1930: S Dimberline
1929: Mr Elmer
1928: A Hackford
1926: A Wood

Brian Hardeman refereed finals 25 years apart, in 1983 and 2008

1925: C Wood
1924: DR Proctor
1923: W Clamp
1922: E Smith
1921: EH Smith
1919: W Cook
1917-16: No competition
1911: W Jones
1910: J Hastie
   GP Cowan, W Winstanley
1907: HP Lewis
1906: Fred Bye
   A Brunt, W Winstanley
1905: Fred Bye
1904: J Fox
1902: J Fox
1901: J Fox
1900: No competition
1897: George H Parkin
(other years, not known)

Mick Poole refereed the 2020 final with his team of Malcolm Levitt, Roger Webb and John Nicolson, pictured alongside the captains of Swinton Athletic (Owen Fieldsend) and Westville (Kieran Hurst)

Mascots

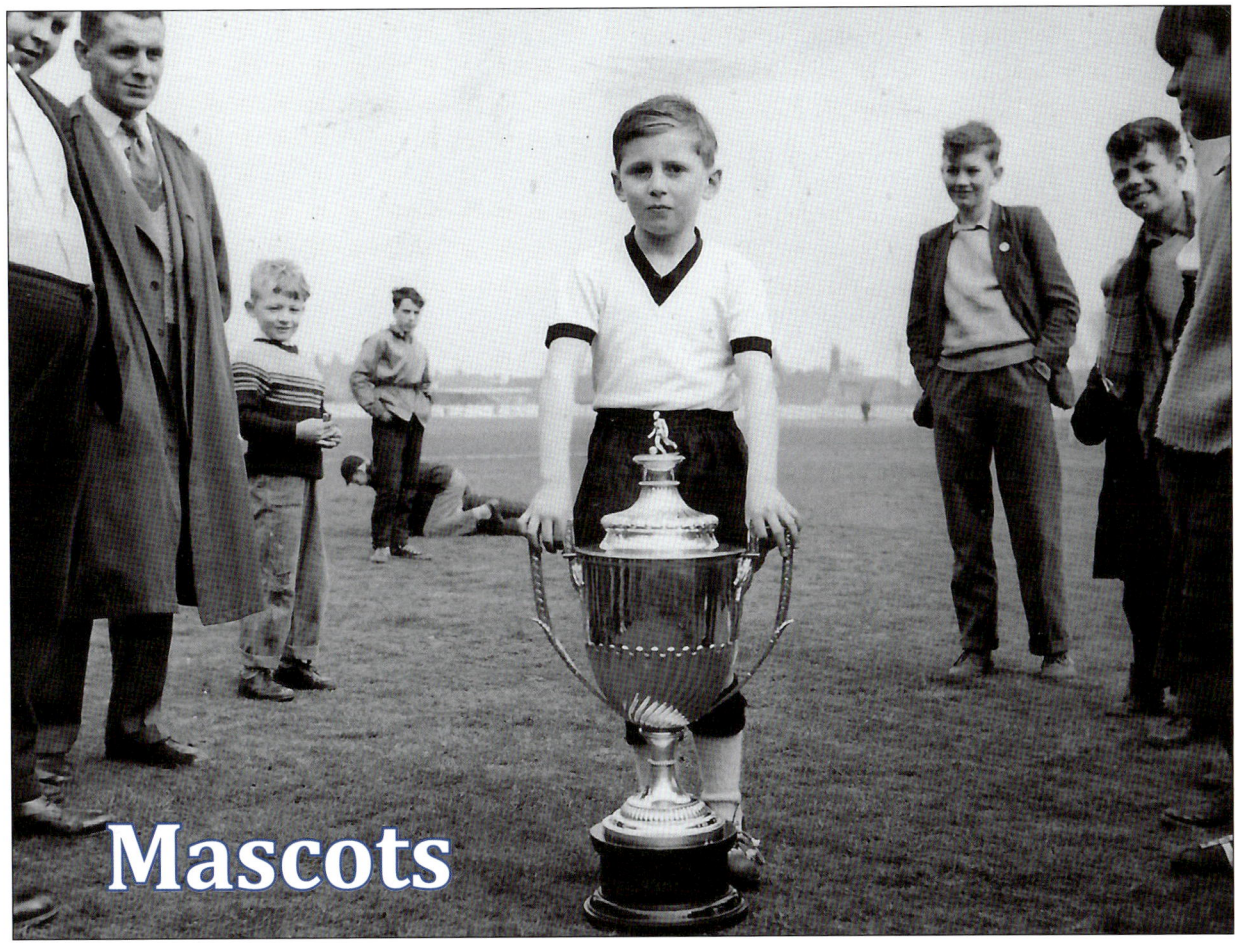

Ford United mascot Chris Rodgers with the Mont after his dad's team's 1960 victory against Houghton Main

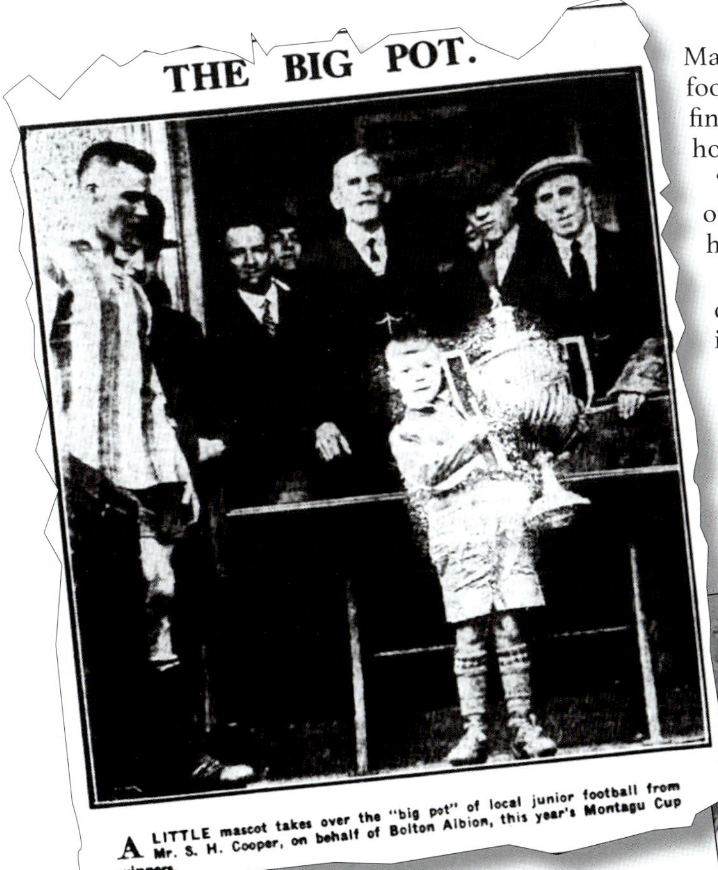

THE BIG POT.

A LITTLE mascot takes over the "big pot" of local junior football from Mr. S. H. Cooper, on behalf of Bolton Albion, this year's Montagu Cup winners.

Mascots are not a new addition to the pre-match football scene. As far back as the 1910s, Montagu Cup finalists gave them the honour of joining their team, hoping the youngsters would bring them extra luck.

'Bower' was given the honour of receiving the Mont on behalf of Bolton Albion in 1929, although did not have the dignity of having his first name revealed!

Chris Rodgers got to pose with the Mont after his dad Tony's Montagu Cup final win for Ford United in 1960.

Denaby United, the 1915 winners, had infants on show with their silverware, while 1937 victors Northcliffe held aloft both their mascot Walter Reeve and the Mont.

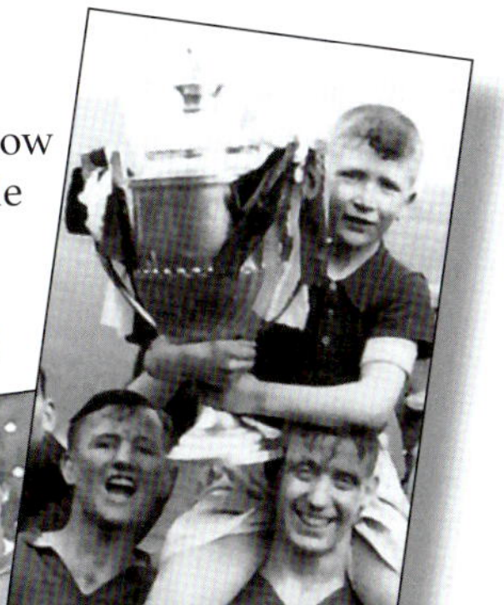

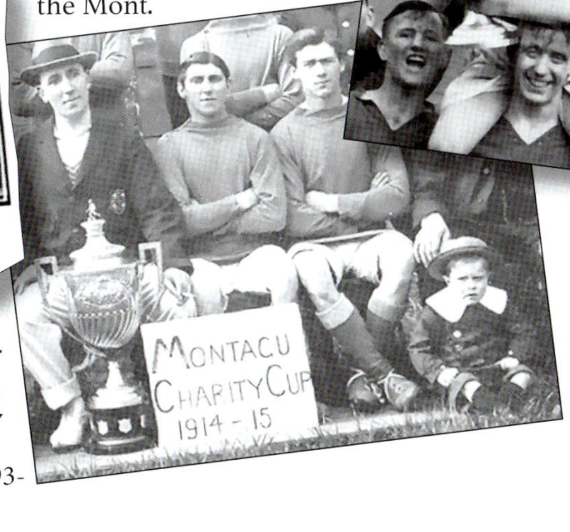

Bolton Albion's 'little mascot' Bower receives the 'big pot' from Mr SM Cooper in 1929, above, and, right, youth is prominent in 1915 and 1937

Publicity

The Mont in the media

The last few years have seen the Mont story take on wings as various branches of the media have discovered the competition.

National and continental magazines, as well as local and regional newspapers, ran stories about the cup and even Yorkshire TV jumped on board.

Here are a few of the features from the Rotherham Advertiser, Doncaster Free Press, Around Town, Football Weekends and Groundtastic magazine.

THE NON-LEAGUE SCENE

THE FULL MONT

Main photo: A tent in the sunshine at Mexborough. Right: The impressive trophy. Insets for fans in the stand, the players celebrate.

STEVE PENNY

...think of it as their own World ...and in a small area of South ...shire, bordered by Barnsley, ...caster and Rotherham, the 'Mont' ...been the centrepiece of their ...balling since 1897.

...Mexborough Montagu Hospital ...y Cup, to give it its full name, ...brates its 125th anniversary next ...and, despite it not being known ...ide that small area, it really does ...e a World Cup link.

...Mont's little brother, the Totty ...a competition covering a ...lar geographical area for primary

schools) was won by Brampton Ellis School in 1939 and 1940, kicking off an incredible story for a young lad from West Melton.

George Robledo scored four goals in both those finals and went on to score the winner for Wath Wanderers in the 1944 Mont final. Within seven years the young Chilean immigrant was making a name for himself on a far bigger stage – playing at Wembley for Newcastle United in the 1951 and 1952 FA Cup finals, scoring the winner in the latter. By then, Robledo had already played for his native Chile in the 1950 World Cup final, including a game against England, where his broad Yorkshire accent proved confusing!

'LOCALS THINK OF IT AS THEIR OWN WORLD CUP'

Robledo, as well as his brother Ted, were not the only players to progress from the Mont to greater things. Leeds United and England World Cup winning trainer Les Cocker scored a hat-trick in the 1942 Mont final for Manvers Main, while many others enjoyed successful Football League careers after their appearance in the Mont, including Lionel Smith, who earned six full England caps, and Joe Beresford, an FA Cup winner with Preston North End.

The final is traditionally played at Mexborough's Hampden Road stadium. It's one of the oldest grounds in England and has a long and proud history – albeit one involving a myriad of clubs that have

risen and fallen over the decades.

Signage around the ground and on the stand is now in the name of Mexborough Athletic but no senior club of that name has played here for more than two decades. A variety of town clubs have used the ground though, from Mexborough FC way back in 1884 to Mexborough Town Athletic, who folded in 2001, and the ground has hosted Midland League, Yorkshire League and FA Cup matches during its 130-year-plus history.

Swathes of concrete terracing around three sides of the historic ground means it is easy to picture how it used to hold crowds of 5,000-plus.

One constant has been the Montagu Cup. Most towns used to host charity cup competitions but the majority have fallen by the wayside, however, the Mont goes on and attracted a near-600 crowd for this season's delayed final. Normally played on Easter Monday, the final was put back to the late May Bank Holiday because of coronavirus restrictions, allowing fans to witness the action.

More than 60 teams have their names inscribed on the magnificent trophy, from Doncaster Rovers to the likes of the Swinton Discharged Soldiers & Sailors, Jump Home Guard and Yorkshire Tar Distillers, plus an array of pub, works, social club, village and semi-professional sides.

DAVID BEDDOWS

125th anniversary beckons for football cup with a history of good deeds and prestige

The crowds, the personalities and the tradition

...OTBALL's modern-day superstars ...ht have the money and the fame ...t for every Premier League ace ...re legions of people who play ...for the love of the game. ...teams, Sunday morning pub teams and ...asing numbers of girls and women's ...keep the sport thriving at the grassroots ...stain its working class traditions. ...otball is also rich with history, crammed ...ues and competitions reaching back ...and next year one of the Rotherham ...ng-running cups is about to celebrate its ...niversary.

...exborough Montagu Cup was first played ...nd its finals grew to attract crowds of ...s each Good Friday or Easter Monday to ...support Mexborough's hospital, as the ...on does to this day.

...y story to those battles was a worthy ...agu Cottage Hospital was officially ...n Bank Street in Mexborough with 14

...ence came about with a need for more ...ment being readily available as the num- ...dents in the local industries was increas-

...time, anyone who sustained injuries had ...ed in their own homes with the more ...urt being transported, usually by horse ...e, to the Rotherham or Doncaster Infir- ...e time had come for the establishment ...spital.

...many of the Kilnhurst players ...d in the days before the NHS. ...was the newly established Mexbor- ...ough player called Meakin. ...According to reports, Meakin was kicked and "retaliated with fists". ...After the game, as the Mexborough players and officials were attempting to board their "wagonette", a number of spectators swarmed around and threw large stones and brick ends. ...Three Mexborough players received nasty injuries and it required eight or ten policemen to "prevent further mischief". ...The extent to which the Mexborough Montagu Cup final was becoming a major local event was shown by the number of people turning out to watch it in the 1930s. ...A picture taken on Good Friday morning, 1937, shows cloth-capped people stood several deep in driving snow at Hampden Road to watch Conisbrough Northcliffe and Wombwell Station Lane contest the trophy.

...competition was limited to teams ...mile radius of Mexborough. ...tagu Cup final took place between ...borough, just as it does today. ...tion soon took off, encouraging ...vries that appealed to an increas- ...people. ...ss of the rivalry was shown in the ...1898 which turned into a bizarre af-

...league winners, Doncaster Rovers, ...a disallowed goal for offside. They ...ed by a spectator. ...ame on the Cup twice, in 1901 and

...lenty of good football for the

swelling crowds to enjoy but passions did boil over.

In 1904, Rotherham Town Reserves took on Mexborough Town and fielded a former Mexborough player called Meakin.

There were nearly 3,000 spectators, with the contest providing a £50 "nest egg" for the Montagu Hospital.

Two years later, an astonishing crowd of 4,700

saw Yorkshire Tar Distillers, from Kilnhurst, thrash Bakers 5-0. The final brought in £88 9s 3d for the hospital.

"In those days most people didn't have cars," says modern-day Montagu Cup committee secretary Barrie Dalby.

"People didn't go to Meadowhall for a day out, they stayed local.

"They didn't have the means to travel very far and the Montagu Cup was a big part of the social calendar.

"The crowds were still big in the 1970s. It was only when car ownership and out-of-town shopping places and leisure became more widespread that crowds decreased."

At the 1950 final between Rawmarsh Welfare and Kilnhurst, the match report noted that "the crowd was kept down to 2,500 by the weather."

The appetite for the Montagu Cup was evidently as strong as ever.

While Wombwell Main, Mexborough Main Street and Swinton Athletic hold the record for

At the 1950 final between Rawmarsh Welfare and Kilnhurst Colliery, which went to a replay won by Rawmarsh, the crowd was kept down to 2,500 by the weather.

most Montagu Cup wins, with seven, it has by no means been a Dearne Valley dominated competition.

The once mighty Rawmarsh Welfare appeared in six finals, winning four of them, and Parkgate Welfare also won it four times in 1948, 1953, 1961 and 1962.

Rawmarsh Horse and Jockey lifted the cup in 1973 and more recently, Rotherham Sunday League's two big hitters, AFP and Joker, have prevailed, AFP four times and Joker once.

The 2020 final will pit Joker against last year's champions, Swinton Athletic, who will be gunning for a record eighth "Monty" title.

The cup they will play for is the same one as Ecclesfield and Newhill contested in the very first final back in 1897.

"It is still the original. It has never been re-cast or replaced," says Barrie.

"There has been more than one FA Cup but only one Montagu Cup. That's quite a feat."

Barrie was involved with Denaby United, seeing

them lift the Montagu Cup twice in the 1970s before he was approached to replace the organising committee's retiring secretary in 2004.

He accepted because of the competition's "good work and prestige."

The legacy continues today thanks to the work of the Montagu Cup's small band of organisers and its main sponsors Stelrad, a company based at Swinton.

The coronavirus pandemic meant last year's final between Swinton Athletic and Westville was eventually played behind closed doors in August.

With the crisis not yet over and restrictions still in place, this year's showpiece may have to be put back from its traditional Easter Monday slot even though supporters can be let in.

As Barrie notes: "The objective of the competition is to raise money for the Hospital Comforts Fund. Playing behind closed doors doesn't achieve that."

As the Montagu Cup approaches its 125th anniversary, organisers want to mark the milestone in

a suitable manner and local football historian and Montagu Cup supporter Chris Brook would welcome any memorabilia from past finals.

The competition's future though depends on the continuing dedication of the people who run it – and upon new faces joining them.

Adds Barrie: "We need younger people to come forward and get involved because we are only a very small committee and all of us are of an 'age', we are no longer youngsters. You have to hand the baton over at some stage."

Although crowds at Montagu Cup finals are counted in much smaller numbers than in years gone by, its pull for local football lovers endures.

Added Barrie: "The Montagu Cup has so much history and even to this day it is still a tradition for many people to go to a Montagu Cup final even though they have no connection to the two finalists."

Anyone with photographs and memorabilia from past Mexborough Montagu Cup finals is welcome to contact Chris Brook on 07985 902346.

MADE OF TOUGH STUFF... rows of flat-capped spectators brave a blizzard at the 1937 Mexborough Montagu Cup final at Hampden Road, Mexborough. Attendances into the thousands were commonplace in the competition's heyday.

CHAMPIONS... Rawmarsh Welfare players and supporters outside the Horse and Jockey pub in 1950 with the Mexborough Montagu Hospital Cup and the Rotherham Charity Cup. Right: Swinton Athletic win the Montagu Cup in 1972.

BENEFICIARY... the old Montague Cottage Hospital. The building was provided and at a long lease by a Mr Andrew Montagu. The Montagu Cup helped support its funding in the days before the NHS and still supports the Hospital Comforts Fund today.

MODERN DAY... Curtis and Alex Wilkinson of 2020 champions Swinton Athletic with their dad Shaun – a three-time Mont winner – chosen by sponsors Stelrad to present the trophy.

Notable players

WILLIAM "DUTCH" GLADWIN
Gladwin (holding the ball in the picture above) was the earliest recorded scorer in a Mexborough Montagu Cup final when he netted in the 1898 showpiece for Kilnhurst. One of six brothers, he signed for Doncaster Rovers soon after but lost his life in December, 1915, at Gallipoli in World War One.

WILF RACE 
Won the Montagu Cup three times player and four times manager.
As a player he won in 1983, 1984 and 1987, each time for Mexborough Main Street.
As a manager won the Mont three times on the bounce in 1995, 1996 and 1997 with Denaby & Cadeby Miners' Welfare, before raising the cup a seventh time in 2006 with Conyers. Wilf is now chairman of Maltby Main.

LIONEL SMITH 
A cultured defender who eschewed "hoofing" the ball up the pitch, Smith played in the 1939 Montagu Cup final when Kilnhurst's Yorkshire Tar Distillers beat Bakers 5-0. A few months later he was playing for Arsenal! Born in Mexborough, Smith turned out 162 times for the Gunners and won six England caps.

LES SWALES
In 1950 Swales managed the remarkable feat of scoring hat-tricks in the finals of both the Montagu Cup and the equally prestigious Rotherham Charity Cup.
He also managed a hat-trick of Montagu Cup wins in 1949, 1950 and 1951 with Rawmarsh Welfare, although 1949 was shared with Kilnhurst Colliery. His sons, Les and John, were also notable local footballers.
John played two matches in one noon in 1978 – starting BSC Parkgate County Senior match and then coming on in the second half of Denaby United's Montagu Cup semi-final.

Corner cutting

ORGANISERS came up with a novel way to settle the 1948 final.
With Manvers Main and Broomhill still level after extra-time, the committee decided that whichever team earned the next corner kick would win the Cup. Five minutes later, Manvers won the next corner and were crowned the champions.

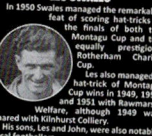

Making history

Wembley and Europe

Mont winners went on to enjoy success at all levels of the game. Several gained international honours, one played at a World Cup finals and many won Football League titles and FA Cups.

However, it was not only at the highest level that Mont 'Old Boys' excelled, as David Beddows, of the *Rotherham Advertiser*, reports:

Colin Dawson won his third Montagu Cup when he represented Rawmarsh Horse & Jockey in 1973 and Pete Scott scored in that final against Rawmarsh Welfare.

The pair went on to win a cup final at Wembley, competed in Europe, got to the third round of the FA Cup... and trained on a field in Rotherham.

Matlock Town, one of the most successful non-league sides of the 1970s, might have been based in Derbyshire but they had South Yorkshire stamped right through them.

Seven of their team that won the FA Trophy at Wembley in 1975 were from Rotherham and the town's playing contingent remained right through the club's glory years, which included knocking Wigan Athletic and Mansfield Town out of the FA Cup and playing two matches in Italy in an Anglo-Italian cup competition in 1979.

After all those successes, played out in front of thousands of fans, the Matlock team would get together to work on their fitness, not at some fenced off private facility, but at Herringthorpe.

"We trained there all the time," remembers Pete Scott, the centre-forward from Kilnhurst who turned out 418 times for Matlock, scoring 182 goals.

"We'd change at the old leisure centre and just go out and get on with it. We'd be there on Tuesdays and Thursdays if we hadn't got a match in midweek and afterwards we'd have a drink at the Park Hotel."

The venue for the sessions, which moved to the floodlit hard courts above

Pete Scott polishes his boots, watched by Colin Dawson, before Matlock's FA Trophy final at Wembley

Herringthorpe Stadium in the winter, made sense because it was convenient for most of the team.

The Rotherham men included the three Fenoughty brothers — Tom, Mick and Nick — Brian Stuart and Colin Oxley, from Dinnington. Another member of the side, Dave Fell, was a local dentist and defender Colin Dawson was from Swinton.

Known as The Gladiators, Matlock played in the Northern Premier League but it was in the cups that they made the biggest headlines.

A trip to Italy was still far from the players' thoughts when they beat Scarborough 4-0 to win the FA Trophy at Wembley in 1975.

> 'After all those successes, played out in front of thousands of fans, the Matlock team would get together to work on their fitness, not at some fenced off private facility, but at Herringthorpe'

"We'd have played at Wembley for nothing. It was a fantastic day," said Colin, who scored one of the goals on what was his 27th birthday.

"I'd never even been to London before that," admitted his friend and Matlock team-mate Pete Scott. "It was a really hot day and the next morning we went around Matlock with the cup on an open-top bus."

That same season, helped by those sweat sessions at Herringthorpe, the Gladiators got through the

qualifying rounds of the FA Cup to play Blackburn Rovers in the first round.

In 1976/77 they beat Wigan Athletic in the first round before thumping Mansfield Town, soon to become Third Division champions, 5-2 in front of more than 8,000 at Field Mill. Matlock went out at Carlisle United in the third round but had momentum – and spirit.

"There were no cliques in that team," remembers Colin. "Nobody thought they were better than anyone else. We all mingled together. It was just like a family club. To think, me and Pete were playing in the Mexborough Montagu Cup in 1973 and then at Wembley in '75. That's a big jump."

An even bigger one was to follow. In 1978 Matlock beat Boston United at Maine Road to win the Northern Premier League Cup – and qualification for an eight-team Anglo-Italian competition.

Shortly after a final training stint at Herringthorpe, the team flew from Heathrow to Italy to play against Pisa and Chieti.

"When we played Pisa, there were 8,000 there," remembers Colin. "At their ground, you emerged from a moat into the stadium, it was like a bowl. There were flares going off in the crowd, we'd never seen anything like it."

Matlock lost both games 2-1 but returned home to host two more Italian teams, Cremonese and Juniorcasale, and beat them both. They just missed out on becoming England's representatives in the final, which was played at the Olympic Stadium in Rome. No wonder Matlock and their home ground, Causeway Lane, was buzzing.

"When we first started playing we had 200 watching. Later on we had 4,000 watching us," remembers Pete.

Pete Scott and Colin Dawson are lauded during Matlock Town's open-top coach tour of the town with the FA Trophy

Matlock's cause was helped by player-manager Peter Swan, the former Sheffield Wednesday and England international. Mick Hennigan, who later worked with Howard Wilkinson in the Football League, was also with Matlock for a while.

The success couldn't last forever.

Matlock had the team but not the facilities to get into the new Alliance Premier League, or "fifth division," introduced in 1979 and as the 1980s dawned the players were entering their 30s.

In 1982 Pete left to join Mexborough and then played with Colin at Swinton Athletic. Retirement beckoned for all.

Colin and Pete were at a reunion of the Matlock team at the Carlton Park Hotel a couple of years ago, reflecting on the glory days and those times running around Herringthorpe.

So was it strange going back to train at Herringthorpe after all those big occasions?

"No," says Pete. "That's just how it was. They were good times. You look back and think: 'we didn't do bad'".

Life as a semi-pro footballer wasn't easy for Matlock's Rotherham contingent. Pete worked down Kilnhurst Colliery and Colin was a bricklayer.

Even after a midweek trip, the players had to be up for work the next morning. They also faced an 80-mile round trip for home games.

"We started out at about £15 a week and after we played at Wembley it went up to £30 to £40, which was a lot of money then," remembers Pete.

"Having said that, we had midweek matches at places like Weymouth, Gateshead and Barrow so you could say we earned it."

Colin added: "After winning the FA Trophy on the Saturday, we had a Derbyshire Cup Final on the Monday and matches on Thursday and Friday to finish the season while working in the day. It was hard work."

Matlock Town's successful squad of the 1970s

The Battle of Highbury

Let battle commence... Stanley Matthews claimed the match against Italy was the most violent of his long career

The "Battle of Highbury" in 1934 was arguably England's most violent match and included four Don & Dearne lads. Indeed two of England's three goals were scored by Mexborough's Eric Brook.

Brook missed a first-minute penalty but was on the scoresheet after three and 10 minutes.

Italy's Luis Monti had sustained a broken foot after a challenge by Ted Drake. Monti played on as the last defender, with the visitors repeatedly retaliating against Drake's second-minute tackle. Eddie Hapgood had his nose broken while Bowden damaged his ankle, Drake was punched and Brook had his arm fractured.

Houghton's Wilf Copping, England's 'hardman', took the man of the match award with a strong fighting and tackling display in midfield. Denaby's Jack Barker and Lionel Smith, of Mexborough, completed the local quartet, who held on for a narrow 3-2 victory against an Italian team who were regarded as heroes and named the 'Lions of Highbury'.

Most of those South Yorkshiremen will have played in the Mont at some time in their careers.

England scored all their three goals in the first 12 minutes against the reigning world champions before defending magnificently in the second half when Italy scored twice and were only denied an equaliser by the woodwork and a series of saves from goalkeeper, Frank Moss.

The FA considered withdrawing from all internationals as a result of the Italians' conduct and Stanley Matthews would later recount that it was the most violent match of his long career.

Afterwards it emerged that the visitors had solid reasons to make an impression. Italian prime minister Benito Mussolini reportedly offered each player an Alfa Romeo car and the equivalent of £150 (more than £6,000 nowadays) to beat the English.

The match saw seven Arsenal players playing in an England shirt, the most a single club has ever supplied to the national team.

The England team ahead of their 1934 clash with Italy

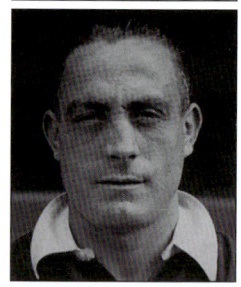

Don & Dearne's finest – from top: Jack Barker, Eric Brook, Wilf Copping and Lionel Smith

Web wise

The Mont on the Net

Keep up to date with any new research about the history of the Montagu Cup.

Competition historian Chris Brook maintains an excellent website, on which this book is largely based.

Any amendments will appear on there, as well as continually updated match results, reports and pictures as the Mont goes on towards its second century.

Mont updates also appear on the competition's Facebook page, with a Twitter page available too.

Chris has also created websites about the Totty Cup and the Barlow-Salmons Shield and is working on a comprehensive summary of Don & Dearne schools football, with a site devoted to the history of the district representative teams.

Add these websites to your favourites!

- *www.montagucup.com*
- *www.facebook.com/montagucup*
- *Twitter: @montagucup*
- *tottycup.co.uk*
- *barlowsalmons.wordpress.com*
- *dondearneschoolfootball.wordpress.com*

Final countdown

1897
Monday, April 9 – Easter Monday
Ecclesfield 2 (Cutts, Hemingfield)
Newhill 0
Hampden Road, Mexborough

1898
Saturday, April 16
Birdwell 2 (not known)
Kilnhurst 1 (William 'Dutch' Gladwin)
Hampden Road, Mexborough.
Attendance: 2,000
Ordered to be replayed after a Kilnhurst complaint
Replay: Saturday, April 30
Kilnhurst 1 (Gladwin)
Birdwell 0
Hampden Road, Mexborough

1899
Monday, April 24
Mexborough 3 (Jagger Holling 2, A Rodgers)
Wath 1 (Smith)
Kilnhurst. Attendance: 1,200

Harry 'Tip' Bennett was the Mexborough captain in 1899

1900
No Montagu Cup played

1901
Saturday, April 6 – Easter Saturday
Doncaster Rovers 5 (Jagger Holling, Manny Lindley, Billy Linward, two not known)
Mexborough Thursday 2 (W Biggs jnr, Theo Collins)
Hampden Road, Mexborough. Attendance: 600

1902
Saturday, March 15
Denaby United 3 (T Hardy, Chadfield, McNeil)
Newhill 0
Hampden Road, Mexborough. Attendance: 1,000

1903
Saturday, March 28
Highthorn 1 (Joss Nevitt)
Wath Athletic 1 (Rogers)
Hampden Road, Mexborough. Attendance: 2,000
Replay: Saturday, April 11 – Easter Saturday
Highthorn 2 (Joss Nevitt, Charlie Bisby)
Wath Athletic 1 (Winstanley)
Hampden Road, Mexborough. Attendance: 1,000

1904
Saturday, March 26
Mexborough Town 4 (Billy Biggs, Roper, Rodgers, R McNeil)
Rotherham Town 1 (Phillip Bratley)
Denaby. Attendance: 1,500

1905
Saturday, April 1
Mexborough Town 1 (Christopher Crapper og)
South Kirkby 0
Bolton-on-Dearne. Attendance: 2,150

1906
Saturday, April 7
Wombwell Main 2 (E Sykes, Powers og)
South Kirkby 1 (Edward Layton)
Hampden Road, Mexborough.
Attendance: 4,000

1907
Saturday, April 13
Kilnhurst Town 2 (Willis Rippon, Jack Burkinshaw)
Parkgate & Rawmarsh 0
Hampden Road, Mexborough

1908
Saturday, April 25
Hickleton Main 3 (Alfred Francis, Gray, S Holland)
Parkgate & Rawmarsh 3 (McGuire, J Ness, A Turner og)
Hampden Road, Mexborough. Attendance: 1,500
Replay: Wednesday, April 29
Hickleton Main 3 (F Law, Alfred Francis, Holling/Holland?)
Parkgate & Rawmarsh 1 (McGuire)
Attendance: 1,000

1909
Saturday, April 10 – Easter Saturday
Goldthorpe Institute 1 (Brazil)
Parkgate & Rawmarsh 1 (Russell)
Wath. Attendance: 1,500
Replay: Friday, April 16
Goldthorpe Institute 3 (Revil, Ryalls, Brazil)
Parkgate & Rawmarsh 1 (Angel)
Hampden Road, Mexborough. Attendance: 1,500

1910
Saturday, April 30
Hickleton Main 2 (McKenning 2)
Mexborough Reserves 0
Bolton-on-Dearne. Attendance: 1,000

1911
Saturday, April 8
Hickleton Main 1 (Murphy)
Ryecroft Wesleyans 1 (T Sutton)
Hampden Road, Mexborough. Attendance: 2,000
Replay: Friday, April 14 – Good Friday
Hickleton Main 3 (Jack Eades 2, Leonard)
Ryecroft Wesleyans 1 (Russell)
Hampden Road, Mexborough

1912
Tuesday, March 28
Hickleton Main 2 (not known)
Frickley Colliery 0
Wath

1913
Monday, April 28
Doncaster Rovers 3 (not known)
Hickleton Main 0
   match abandoned, bad weather
Wednesday, April 30
Doncaster Rovers 3 (Tommy Astill, Shackleton, Jack Nuttall)
Hickleton Main 0
Hampden Road, Mexborough

Sid Dawson scored four times in the 1914 final for Kilnhurst

1914
Saturday, April 11 – Easter Saturday
Kilnhurst Town 6 (Sid Dawson 4, J Clarke 2)
South Yorkshire Hotel (Mexborough) 1 (Ferguson)
Hampden Road, Mexborough

1915
Saturday, April 17
Denaby United 2 (Jepson, Owen Bransby)
Mexborough Grand Central Loco 2 (Glennon, Atkins)
Hampden Road, Mexborough.
Replay: Saturday, May 1
Denaby United 2 (Owen Bransby, Jepson)
Mexborough Grand Central Loco 0

1916
No competition – World War One

1917
No competition – World War One

1918
Saturday, May 11
Mexborough Rovers 1 (not known)
Denaby Mission 1 (not known)
Hampden Road, Mexborough
Two more drawn replays were played, result and scorers not known:
Saturday, May 18 and Tuesday, May 21
3rd Replay: Saturday, May 25
Mexborough Rovers 2 (Hackford, Percy Beaumont)
Denaby Mission 0
Denaby

1919
Monday, April 21 – Easter Monday
Kimberworth Old Boys 2 (Wightman, George Dobson)
Denaby United 1 (Garthwaite)
Hampden Road, Mexborough. Attendance: 1,800

1920
Saturday, April 5 – Easter Monday
Swinton Discharged Soldiers & Sailors 1 (V Temple)
Swinton Church 0
Hampden Road, Mexborough. Attendance: 3,000

1921
Saturday, March 28 – Easter Monday
Parkgate Christ Church 1 (Harry Maycock)
Barnburgh Colliery 0
Hampden Road, Mexborough. Attendance: 1,850

1922
Tuesday, April 18
Barnburgh Colliery 1 (Marshall)
Swinton Discharged Soldiers & Sailors 1 (Foster)
Hampden Road, Mexborough. Attendance: 1,800
Replay: Monday, April 24
Barnburgh Colliery 4 (Bullock, Hardwick, Marshall, Spencer)
Swinton Discharged Soldiers & Sailors 3 (Wingfield 2, Reader)
Hampden Road, Mexborough

1923
Tuesday, April 3 – Easter Tuesday)
Kilnhurst WMC 3 (W Chappel, W Goodby, Tommy Frith)
Sandhill Juniors 3 (F Wilde 2, A Bennett)
Hampden Road, Mexborough
Replay: Saturday, April 28
Kilnhurst WMC 4 (W Chappel, W Goodby, Tommy Frith, C Saxton)
Sandhill Juniors 1 (A Hopkinson)
Hampden Road, Mexborough. Attendance: 1,500

1924
Friday, April 18 – Good Friday
Askern Road WMC 3 (Bennison, F Bryant, Joe Beresford)
Kilnhurst WMC 1 (Tommy Frith)
Hampden Road, Mexborough.

1925
Friday, April 10 – Good Friday
Darfield Bridge 3 (Mynett, Tyler, Roberts)
South Elmsall United Services 2 (Martin, McGuire)
Hampden Road, Mexborough. Attendance: 1,000+

1926
Friday, April 2 – Good Friday
Darfield Bridge 1 (Smallman)
Goldthorpe United 0
Hampden Road, Mexborough

1927
Friday, April 15 – Good Friday
Goldthorpe United 3 (Hadlington 2, Goodman)
South Yorkshire Chemical Works 0
Hampden Road, Mexborough. Attendance: 3,000

1928
Friday, April 6 – Good Friday
Ashwood Road WMC 0
Roman Terrace 0
Hampden Road, Mexborough
Replay: Wednesday, April 25
Ashwood Road WMC 2 (Wrack, Bailey)
Roman Terrace 1 (Hepworth)
Hampden Road, Mexborough

1929
Friday, March 29 – Good Friday
Bolton Albion 2 (George Walker 2)
Conisbrough Welfare 0
Hampden Road, Mexborough. Attendance: 2,000

1930
Friday 18th April (Good Friday)
Goldthorpe United 1 (Skitt og)
Halfway House 1 (Lunness)
Hampden Road, Mexborough
Replay: Friday, May 2
Goldthorpe United 3 (Denman, Frank Chivers, S Chivers)
Halfway House 1 (Netherwood)
Hampden Road, Mexborough. Attendance: 2,300

1931
Friday, April 3 – Good Friday
Goldthorpe United 1 (Riley)
Broomhill 0
Wath. Attendance: 2,000

1932
Friday, March 25 – Good Friday
Thorpe Hesley 2 (Hague, own goal)
Thurnscoe Vics 2 (Mace 2)
Wath. Attendance: 5,000
Replay: Saturday, April 9
Thorpe Hesley 3 (Sylvester 2, Ashton)
Thurnscoe Vics 1 (Mace)
Wath. Attendance: 3,000

1933
Friday, April 14 – Good Friday
Thurnscoe Vics 1 (Whitehead)
Cudworth Village 0
Wath. Attendance: 3,500

1934
Friday, March 30 – Good Friday
Mexborough Athletic 2 (Roome, Moxon)
Silverwood 0
Wath

1935
Friday, April 19 – Good Friday
Cudworth St Mary's 6 (George Blenkinsop 2, Paddy Poole 2, Charlie Corns, Sam Turnock)
Wath Main 1 (Scattergood)
Wath

1936
Friday, April 10 – Good Friday
Wath Road Athletic 3 (Cyril Jeavons, Cotton, Clegg)
Rawmarsh Welfare 1 (Albert Unwin)
Wath. Attendance: 2,000

1937
Friday, March 26 – Good Friday
Northcliffe WMC 4 (Tait 2, Carte, Barnes)
Wombwell Station Lane 1 (Prescott)
Hampden Road, Mexborough. Attendance: 2,800

1938
Friday, April 15 – Good Friday
Thurnscoe Vics 3 (Rowe, Mace, Routledge)
Silverwood 0
Hampden Road, Mexborough

1939
Friday, April 7 – Good Friday
Yorkshire Tar Distillers 5 (Jack Burkinshaw 2, Arthur Vickers, Steve Vickers, South)
Baker & Bessemers 0
Hampden Road, Mexborough. Attendance: 4,700

1940
Friday, March 22 – Good Friday
Manvers Main 8 (C Grant 3, Stan Burton 2, W Deakin, Cyril Warren, Harry Newey)
Grimethorpe Rovers 0
Hampden Road, Mexborough. Attendance: 3,868

1941
Monday, April 14 – Easter Monday
Manvers Main 2 (F Betts 2)
Grimethorpe Rovers 1 (Rayner)
Hampden Road, Mexborough

Albert Horner won three Montagu Cups with Manvers in 1941, 42 and 45

1942
Week beginning May 16
Manvers Main 4 (John Cocker 3, Chambers og)
Upton Colliery 2 (Harper, Fowler)
Denaby

1943
Monday, April 26
New Stubbin Colliery 2 (Dixon, Perkins)
Old Mill (South Kirkby) 1 (Sidebottom)
Hampden Road, Mexborough

1944
Monday, April 10 – Easter Monday
Wath Wanderers 3 (Davies 2, Morgan)
Denaby United 3 (Gibbs 2, Moralee)
Hampden Road, Mexborough. Attendance: 5,704
Replay: Saturday, April 29
Wath Wanderers 2 (George Robledo, Raynor)
Denaby United 1 (Wally Ardron)

1945
Saturday (possibly March 30)
Manvers Main 1 (Barlow)
Broomhill Boys 1 (Dennis Moreton)
Wath
Manvers Main won on the 'next corner wins' ruling, during extra-time.

1946
Friday, April 19 – Good Friday
Kilnhurst 2 (Billy Deakin, Frank Adey)
Shipcroft United 1 (Woodcock)
Hampden Road, Mexborough. Attendance: 3,000

1947
Saturday, May 17
Jump Home Guard 3 (T Outram, Horsfield, Ibberson)
New Stubbin Colliery 2 (not known)
Rawmarsh

Jump Home Guard players with the 1947 Montagu Cup

1948
Saturday, April 10
Parkgate Welfare 2 (Dougie Page, Ralph Whitworth)
Jump Home Guard 1 (Ibberson)
Hampden Road, Mexborough

1949
Monday, April 18 – Easter Monday
Rawmarsh Welfare 1 (Charlie Ardron)
Kilnhurst Colliery 1 (George Frith)
Hampden Road, Mexborough. Attendance: 3,600
Replay: Saturday, May 7
Rawmarsh Welfare 0
Kilnhurst Colliery 0
Denaby – Cup shared

1950
Monday, April 10 – Easter Monday
Rawmarsh Welfare 2 (Colin Chaplin, Charlie Ardron)
Kilnhurst Colliery 2 (Les Harpham, George Frith)
Hampden Road, Mexborough. Attendance: 2,528
Replay: Wednesday, April 19
Rawmarsh Welfare 3 (Swales 3)
Kilnhurst Colliery 1 (not known)
Hampden Road, Mexborough

1951
Date not known
Rawmarsh Welfare 2 (Les Swales, Dawson og)
Bowbroom WMC 1 (Hallam)
Match abandoned – bad weather
Restaging: Saturday, May 5
Rawmarsh Welfare 2 (Les Swales 2)
Bowbroom WMC 1 (Geoff Priestley)
Hampden Road, Mexborough. Attendance: 1,000

1952
Monday, April 14 – Easter Monday
Silverwood Colliery 2 (Trickett, Edwards)
Denaby Rovers 2 (Whitehead, Sapey)
Hampden Road, Mexborough
Replay: Monday, April 28
Silverwood Colliery 3 (not known)
Denaby Rovers 0

1953
Monday, April 6 – Easter Monday
Parkgate Welfare 2 (Aubrey Morris, Albert Gillott)
Dragon United 1 (Whitehead)
Denaby

1954
Monday, April 19 – Easter Monday
Silverwood Colliery 1 (Gordon Rowlands)
Bolton Ings Lane 0
Hampden Road, Mexborough. Attendance: 3,062

1955
Monday, April 11 – Easter Monday
Denaby United 2 (Austin, Davies)
Bowbroom WMC 0
Hampden Road, Mexborough. Attendance: 4,740

1956
Monday, April 2 – Easter Monday
Dearne MW 2 (Cyril Roebuck 2)
Mexborough Schofield Tech Coll Old Boys 1 (Don Lancashire)
Denaby. Attendance: 2,697

1957
Monday, April 22 – Easter Monday
Mexborough Schofield TCOB 3 (Ken Lee, Ken King, Brian Dutton)
Hickleton Main 2 (Heathcock, Tarmey)
Hampden Road, Mexborough. Attendance: 1,500

1958
Monday, April 7 – Easter Monday
Bowbroom WMC 2 (Shudda Mitchell, Stan Hoyland)
Denaby United 0
Hampden Road, Mexborough. Attendance: 2,671

1959
Monday, March 30 – Easter Monday
Tom Hill Old Boys 4 (Glyn Watkin, Howard Stockwell, Pete Dyson, Richard Marston)
Denaby Rovers 1 (Sapey)
Hampden Road, Mexborough. Attendance: 3,000

1960
Monday, April 18 – Easter Monday
Ford United 4 (Freddie Gilbert 2, Roy Shepherd, Arthur Wright)
Houghton Main 0
Hampden Road, Mexborough. Attendance: 2,745

1961
Monday, April 3 – Easter Monday
Parkgate Welfare 4 (Peter Bentley 2, Terry Staniforth 2)
Ford United 3 (D Marston, Freddie Gilbert, Don Morgan)
Hampden Road, Mexborough. Attendance: 2,343

1962
Monday, April 23 – Easter Monday
Parkgate Welfare 2 (Staniforth, Harold Dungworth)
Houghton Main 0
Hampden Road, Mexborough. Attendance: 1,865

1963
Monday, April 15 – Easter Monday
Maltby Miners Welfare 5
  (Griffiths 2, Tony Fallon,
  Green, Shaw)
Tom Hill Old Boys 1 (own goal)
Hampden Road, Mexborough.
Attendance: 1,850

1964
Monday, March 30 – Easter Monday
Swinton Athletic 7
  (Marshall Robshaw 3,
  Brian Hyde 2, Melvyn Senior,
  Tony Grant
Silverwood Colliery 1
  (Brian Liversidge)
Hampden Road, Mexborough.
Attendance: 1,188

1965
Monday, April 19 – Easter Monday
Dearne Miners Welfare 3 (Dave Cocksedge 2,
  Frank Smallwood)
Maltby Main 1 (Neil Ramsey)
Hampden Road, Mexborough. Attendance: 1,904

1966
Monday, April 11 – Easter Monday
High Terrace 2 (Tommy Law, Bill Cotton)
Maltby Miners Welfare 2 (Neil Ramsey 2)
Hampden Road, Mexborough. Attendance: 2,161
Replay: Sunday, April 24
High Terrace 5 (Peter Davies 3, Arthur Jones 2)
Maltby Miners Welfare 1 (Green)
Hampden Road, Mexborough. Attendance: 1,500

1967
Monday, March 27 – Easter Monday
High Terrace 1 (Les Dalton og)
Denaby United 0
Hampden Road, Mexborough. Attendance: 3,655

1968
Monday, April 15 – Easter Monday
Swinton Athletic 2 (Malc Whitehouse,
  Colin Whitehouse)
High Terrace 0
Hampden Road, Mexborough. Attendance: 3,943

1969
Sunday, April 6 – Easter Sunday
Houghton Main 4 (J Pilkington 2, J Guest,
  D Blayden
East Dene 2 (Edwards 2)
Hampden Road, Mexborough. Attendance: 2,000

1970
Monday, March 30 – Easter Monday
Denaby United 0
Northcliffe WMC 0
Hampden Road, Mexborough. Attendance: 2,628
Replay: Sunday, May 3
Denaby United 1 (Roger Willey)
Northcliffe WMC 0
Hampden Road, Mexborough. Attendance: 1,097

1966 winners High Terrace kept their hands on the Mont the following year

1971
Monday, April 12 – Easter Monday
Northcliffe WMC 1 (George Laycock)
Houghton Main 0
Hampden Road, Mexborough. Attendance: 2,300

1972
Monday, April 3 – Easter Monday
Swinton Athletic 6 (Malc Whitehouse 2,
  John Wheeler 2, Norman Adey 2)
Northcliffe WMC 0
Hampden Road, Mexborough. Attendance: 2,800

1973
Monday, April 23 – Easter Monday
Rawmarsh Horse & Jockey 1 (Pete Scott)
Rawmarsh Welfare 1 (Pete Roddis)
Hampden Road, Mexborough
Replay: Sunday, May 13
Rawmarsh Horse & Jockey 1 (Dave Cousins)
Rawmarsh Welfare 0
Hampden Road, Mexborough

1974
Monday, April 15 – Easter Monday
Denaby United 1 (Pete Pettit)
Jungle United 1 (Charlie Green)
Hampden Road, Mexborough
Replay: Sunday, May 5
Denaby United 2 (Frank Morley 2)
Jungle United 1 (Derek Neal)
Hampden Road, Mexborough

1975
Monday, March 31 – Easter Monday
Houghton Main 3 (John Pilkington,
  Tommy Gregory, John Smith)
Northcliffe WMC 2 (Jimmy Noonan 2)
Hampden Road, Mexborough. Attendance: 1,616

1976
Monday, April 19 – Easter Monday
Rawmarsh Welfare 3 (Mick Farley, John Cooke,
  Brian Turton og)
Swinton Athletic 1 (Neil Spencer)
Hampden Road, Mexborough. Attendance: 3,000

1977
Monday, April 11 – Easter Monday
Mexborough Town 2 (Pete Pettit, Ian Smith)
Edlington WMC 1 (Cyril Parker)
Hampden Road, Mexborough. Attendance: 2,500

1978
Monday, March 27 – Easter Monday
Denaby United 4 (Bob Mountain 2, Allan Craw 2)
Houghton Main 2 (Dave Lyman, Tommy Gregory)
Hampden Road, Mexborough. Attendance: 2,000

1979
Monday, April 16 – Easter Monday
Northgate WMC 1 (Bernard Coop)
BSC Parkgate 0
Hampden Road, Mexborough

1980
Monday, April 7 – Easter Monday
Swinton Athletic 3 (Alan Taylor, Glyn Whitehouse, John Cook)
Edlington WMC 0
Hampden Road, Mexborough. Attendance: 3,000+

1981
Monday, April 20 – Easter Monday
Maltby Miners Welfare 0
Mexborough Main Street 0
Hampden Road, Mexborough. Attendance: 2,000+
Replay: Monday, April 27
Maltby Miners Welfare 1 (Richard Moon)
Mexborough Main Street 0
Hampden Road, Mexborough? Attendance: 1,000

1982
Monday, April 12 – Easter Monday
Dearne CMW 3 (Jeff Earnshaw 2, John Weaver)
Rotherham Club 1 (Nigel Sharp)
Hampden Road, Mexborough. Attendance: 2,000

1983
Monday, April 4 – Easter Monday
Mexborough Main Street 2 (Gary Skidmore, Wilf Race)
Northcliffe WMC 0
Hampden Road, Mexborough. Attendance: 2,500

1984
Monday, April 23 – Easter Monday
Mexborough Main Street 2 (Les Oxer, Jeff Earnshaw)
Goldthorpe Colliery 1 (Barry Walker)
Hampden Road, Mexborough. Attendance: 1,700

1985
Monday, April 8 – Easter Monday
Northgate WMC 3 (Gary Lindsay 2, Dean Oxer)
New Stubbin Colliery 0
Hampden Road, Mexborough. Attendance: 1,400

1986
Monday, March 31 – Easter Monday
Swinton Athletic 2 (Colin Seaman, Stevie Johnson)
Mexborough Main Street 0
Hampden Road, Mexborough. Attendance: 2,500

Ian 'Ike' Cotton, pictured with son Robbie, was a scorer in the 1987 and 1998 finals for Mexborough Main Street

1987
Monday, April 20 – Easter Monday
Mexborough Main Street 4 (Ian Cotton 2, Jeff Earnshaw, Neil Winfield)
BSC Parkgate 2 (Paul Cooke, Peter Ward)
Hampden Road, Mexborough. Attendance: 2,000

1988
Monday, April 4 – Easter Monday
Denaby & Cadeby Miners Welfare 2 (Ian Smith, Gary Smith)
Swinton Athletic 1 (Paul Hyde)
Hampden Road, Mexborough. Attendance: 1,500

1989
Monday, March 27 – Easter Monday
Swinton Athletic 2 (John Hodgson, Don Elliott)
Wath Saracens 1 (Gary Moody)
Hampden Road, Mexborough. Attendance: 2,000+

1990
Monday, April 16 – Easter Monday
Goldthorpe Colliery 2 (Dave Salkeld, Russ Towning)
Inferno Fire Protection 0
Hampden Road, Mexborough. Attendance: 1,500

1991
Monday, April 1 – Easter Monday
Denaby & Cadeby Miners Welfare 2 (Gary Smith, Doug Hughes og)
Swinton Athletic 1 (Andy Mangham)
Hampden Road, Mexborough

1992
Monday, April 20 – Easter Monday
Brodsworth Miners Welfare 2 (Darren Wedlock, Rankine)
RES Parkgate 1 (Neil Stringer)
Hampden Road, Mexborough

1993
Monday, April 12 – Easter Monday
Brodsworth Miners Welfare 1 (Bill Hancock)
Goldthorpe Colliery 1 (Gary Hough)
Hampden Road, Mexborough
Replay: Thursday 29th April
Brodsworth Miners Welfare 2 (Gary Cygan, Paul Dodge)
Goldthorpe Colliery 0
Tickhill Square, Denaby Main

1994
Monday, April 4 – Easter Monday
Wath St James 1 (Shaun Temple)
Goldthorpe Colliery 0
Hampden Road, Mexborough

1995
Monday, April 17 – Easter Monday
Denaby & Cadeby Miners Welfare 2 (Dean Oxer, Paul Cooke)
Mexborough Main Street 0
Hampden Road, Mexborough

1996
Monday, April 8 – Easter Monday
Denaby & Cadeby Miners Welfare 4 (Paul Cooke, John Hemmingway, Ian Smith, Paul Harper)
Wath Saracens 2 (John Ransford, Andrew Price og)
Hampden Road, Mexborough

1997
Monday, March 31 – Easter Monday
Denaby & Cadeby Miners Welfare 2 (Jamie Robshaw, Stuart Dudhill)
Wath Saracens 1 (Barry Davies)
Hampden Road, Mexborough

1998
Monday, April 13 – Easter Monday
Wombwell Main 3 (Andy Gay, Chris Birks, Ian Woodall)
Mexborough Main Street 2 (Ian Cotton, Chris France)
Hampden Road, Mexborough

1999
Monday, April 5 – Easter Monday
Mexborough Main Street 2 (Neil Sigsworth, Darren Clegg)
Denaby United 2 (Ian Newey, Scott Mason)
Hampden Road, Mexborough. Attendance: 1,500
Replay: Thursday, April 22
Mexborough Main Street 1 (Karl Kent)
Denaby United 0
Hampden Road, Mexborough. Attendance: 500

2000
Monday, April 24 – Easter Monday
Mexborough Main Street 1 (Dean Oxer)
Denaby United 0
Hampden Road, Mexborough

2001
Monday, April 16 – Easter Monday
Wombwell Main 2 (Lee Brooks 2)
Edlington Working Men's Club 0
Hampden Road, Mexborough.
Attendance: 500

2002
Monday, April 1 – Easter Monday
Wombwell Main 2 (Ben Naylor, James Boulton)
Groves Social 1 (Craig Loftus)
Hampden Road, Mexborough.
Attendance: 500

Wombwell Main's Richard Portman with the 2002 Mont

2003
Monday, April 21 – Easter Monday
Wombwell Main 4 (James Boulton 2, Gary Hurst, Andy Smith)
Groves Social 2 (Ryan Scott, Paul Hemmingway)
Hampden Road, Mexborough

2004
Monday, April 12 – Easter Monday
Dearne CMW 2 (Tom Rae, Phil Taylor)
Westville 2 (Jamie Williams, Luke Sykes)
Hampden Road, Mexborough.
Attendance: 700

Replay: Wednesday, April 28
Dearne CMW 6 (Tom Rae 2, Scott Clarke 2, Phil Smith 2)
Westville 1 (Andy Webb og)
Hampden Road, Mexborough

2005
Monday, March 28 – Easter Monday
Mexborough Main Street 2 (Gareth Petch, Mark Nisbet og)
Groves Social 0
Hampden Road, Mexborough.

2006
Monday, April 17 – Easter Monday
Conyers 1 (Rob Oxer)
Houghton Main 1 (Anthony Storey)
Hampden Road, Mexborough

Replay: Thursday, April 20
Conyers 3 (Steven Ellor 2, Paul Hemmingway)
Houghton Main 0
Hampden Road, Mexborough

2007
Monday, April 9 – Easter Monday
Wombwell Main 2 (Scott Smith, Dean Fearon)
Mexborough Main Street 2 (Gavin Allott, Gary Hibbert)
Hampden Road, Mexborough
Replay: Friday, April 27
Wombwell Main 5 (Dean Sidebottom 2, Simon Chadburn, Troy Bennett, Jamie Williams)
Mexborough Main Street 1 (Craig Roden)
Hampden Road, Mexborough

2008
Monday, March 24 – Easter Monday
Mexborough Main Street 3 (Adam Hallsworth, Chris Greaves, Rob Branagan)
Dearne CMW 0
Hampden Road, Mexborough

2009
Monday, April 13 – Easter Monday
Wombwell Main 4 (Troy Bennett 2, Mark Harling, Craig Rouse)
Westville 0
Hampden Road, Mexborough

2010
Monday, April 5 – Easter Monday
Groves Social 2 (Steven Ellor 2)
Wombwell Main 1 (Martin Watkin)
Hampden Road, Mexborough. Attendance: 450

2011
Monday, April 25 – Easter Monday
Swinton WMC 2 (Brett Lovell, Ricky License)
Houghton Main 1 (Josh Moore)
Hampden Road, Mexborough. Attendance: 600

2012
Monday, April 9 – Easter Monday
AFP 1 (Andrew Haythorne)
Swinton WMC 0
Hampden Road, Mexborough

2013
Monday, April 1 – Easter Monday
AFP 2 (Martin Jones, Gavin Allott)
Swinton WMC 0
Hampden Road, Mexborough

2014
Monday, April 21 – Easter Monday
AFP 1 (Rob Branagan)
Swinton Athletic 0
Hampden Road, Mexborough. Attendance: 550

2015
Monday, April 6 – Easter Monday
Memories 4 (Danny South, Ben Pankovics, Michael Russon, Tommy Needham)
Swinton Athletic 3 (Justin Greenwood 2, Ryan Doxey)
Hampden Road, Mexborough. Attendance: 950

2016
Monday, March 28 – Easter Monday)
AFP 3 (Steven Hopewell 2, Ben Thornton)
Houghton Main 1 (Jake Simon)
Hampden Road, Mexborough

Rob Branagan has played in four finals, including one aged just 17. He scored in both the 2008 and 2014 finals

2017
Monday, April 17 – Easter Monday
Houghton Main 1 (Danny Burkinshaw)
Joker 0
Hampden Road, Mexborough. Attendance: 420

2018
Friday, April 13
Westville 4 (Shawn Mitchell 2, Kieran Hirst, Nicky Harper)
Wombwell Main 0
Hampden Road, Mexborough. Attendance: 450

2019
Monday, April 22 – Easter Monday
Joker 2 (Ryan Smyth, Danny Patterson)
Wombwell Main 0
Match abandoned – serious injury to a Joker player
Restaging: Monday, May 29
Joker 6 (Ross Duggan 4, Steve McDonnell 2)
Wombwell Main 0
Hampden Road, Mexborough

The 2020 Montagu Cup final had to be played behind closed doors due to Covid restrictions. That did not prevent a handful of fans sneaking a peek at the action at Queens United's ground in West Melton

2020
Sunday, August 9
Swinton Athletic 5 (Shawn Mitchell 2, Enzo Guarini, Alex Wilkinson, Curtis Wilkinson)
Westville 2 (Kieran Hirst, Liam Graham)
Queens, West Melton
Attendance: Behind closed doors – Covid-19

2021
Monday, May 31
Swinton Athletic 2 (Matt Thornton 2)
Joker 1 (Joe Austin)
Hampden Road, Mexborough. Attendance 900

2022
Monday, April 18 – Easter Monday
Scawthorpe Athletic 4 (Lee Tilley, Adam Watson, Gaz Mundy, Sam Corner)
Dog Daisy United 3 (Jake Ford 2, Josh Moore)
Hampden Road, Mexborough. Attendance: 1,700

These enterprising Dog Daisy United fans parked their flat-bed pick-up truck next to the wall of Hampden Road to grab a look at the 2021 Covid-restricted semi-final

2023
Monday, April 10 – Easter Monday
Dog Daisy United versus Dearne & District
at Hampden Road, Mexborough.

Dog Daisy's Owen Fieldsend heads their first goal in the semi-final victory against Brinsworth DC to book his team a place in the 2023 final

Lest We Forget...

Don & Dearne's football war heroes

Not all of these played in Montagu Cup finals but many will have played in earlier rounds, as well as for teams who were cup regulars. The list is not comprehensive and we remember all those who fell in service of their country.

Billy Westwood appeared in the 1904 Montagu Cup final. He played for Thornhill United (later Rotherham County), Denaby United, Mexborough Town and Bristol Rovers. He broke his leg playing for Rovers (something that is said to have denied him international honours) after which he rejoined Mexborough Town.

He married a Mexborough girl, Elizabeth Denham, in 1909.

Billy fell while fighting around Arras, France, on May 3, 1917. Born William Howell Powell Westwood, in Dudley in 1886, the corporal served with the 2/5th Battalion King's Own Yorkshire Light Infantry and is commemorated on the Arras Memorial (bay 7) Pas De Calais, France.

Billy's grandson, Dennis Priestley won world darts championship titles in 1991 and 1994.

Joe Smith, from Kilnhurst, won the 1912 Montagu Cup with Hickleton Colliery before playing for Birmingham and then Chesterfield.

He served in the 17th Battalion, Middlesex Regiment – the so-called Footballers' Battalion – in northern France. He rose to the rank of Company Sergeant Major and was killed on November 13, 1916, near the end of the Battle of the Somme. Joe was mentioned in dispatches for displaying considerable bravery "after being wounded, again dashed into battle, only to be shot down".

Born August 23, 1889, he was the son of Benjamin and Maria Smith of Swinton. He is buried in Serre Road Cemetery No.1, Pas De Calais, in plot 1, row G, grave 19 with an inscription that reads: "He died the noblest of death A man may die fighting for God and right liberty."

Charlie Bentham played in previous rounds of the Mont as he got a medal. He was killed in World War One. Badly injured on the first day of the Somme, July 1, 1916, he survived the battlefield only to die three weeks later in Wrexham Hospital aged 26. He is buried just inside the gates of St Thomas Churchyard, Kilnhurst.

Allen Foster, of Rawmarsh played for Parkgate Athletic, before making his name for Reading. He is remembered for a hat-trick scored against Italian giants AC Milan in the Biscuitmen's 5-0 victory in 1914.

The result prompted leading Italian newspaper Corriere della Sera to report that "without doubt, Reading FC are the finest foreign team seen in Italy".

On August 8, 1916, Allen went over the top with the battalion during the Battle of Delville Wood and was shot in the thigh, abdomen and arm. He was recovered by four stretcher-bearers from No Man's Land and transported to a hospital, where he died from his wounds.

He was serving with the 17th Battalion Middlesex Regiment and is buried in the Corbie Communal Cemetery Extension (plot 2, row A, grave 70) Somme, France.

His gravestone inscription reads: "In ever loving remembrance of my dear husband who fell in Delville Wood aged 29yrs. Mrs BE Foster".

Larrett Roebuck, of Jump, played for Silverwood Colliery and then Huddersfield Town. On October 18, 1914, he was recorded as "presumed dead" after an attack during the Race to the Sea. His death was confirmed by two comrades in January 1915. Larrett was the first Football League player to be killed in the First World War.

He was born in Rawmarsh in 1885 and was serving with the 2nd Battalion York and Lancaster Regiment. He has no known grave but is on the Ploegsteert Memorial, panel 8 in Hainaut, Belgium.

William "Dutch" Gladwin, of Kilnhurst, got the winner in the second Montagu Cup final in 1898, before signing for Doncaster Rovers.

He lost his life on May 8, 1915, serving with the 2nd Battalion King's Own Royal Lancaster Regiment. He is remembered on the Ypres Menin Gate, panel 12, in West Flanders, Belgium.

Leslie Thompson, of Little Houghton, was the son of Albert and Gladys May Thompson and played for England Schoolboys. He was only 17 when World War Two started and was already a professional with Leeds United, making 32 appearances. He served in the RAF 630 squadron Volunteer Reserve and was on a Lancaster bomber on a night bombing mission on August 27, 1944. They were attacked by a fighter, which forced their plane to crash in a field in Denmark. Leslie died aged 22 and was buried in Skarrild Churchyard, Denmark.

The other cups

Silverware for all

The Montagu Cup

The Mont is just one of the trophies handed over each year to the winning team in the Montagu Cup final. The Bernard Hodgkinson Memorial Trophy has been presented to the Montagu Cup runners-up since 1983, with the Peter Taylor Memorial Trophy awarded to the man of the match.

The Peter Taylor Memorial Trophy and Bernard Hodgkinson Memorial Trophy flank the magnificent Montagu Cup

Totty Cup

The Totty Cup is a competition for schools, which has been played across the Don & Dearne region since 1923. It celebrates its centenary in 2023.

It was instigated by cinema owner Russell Totty. In the first season it was referred to as the Goldthorpe Picture House Cup before taking its present name the following year. The first final saw Wath Victoria beat Wath Park Road.

In those early days it was senior schools (13 and 14-year-olds) who played. After World War Two the school system changed and it became a primary school trophy. At the same time the Dearne Schools FA merged with the Don Schools FA to become the Don & Dearne Schools FA.

In the 1940s and 1950s, inter-school football was a weekly event. There were so many leagues and cups in the Don & Dearne district that memories are often clouded as to what people won as school children. Brian Blessed, for example, has claimed

Chris Speight, of Circuits Electrical, hands the Totty Cup to Alfie Skidmore, of 2022 winners Swinton Queen Street

on television that he won the Totty Cup with Highgate in 1948 but it must have been a different competition because they did not win it between 1934 and 1956.

Most wins (primary school)
8: Bolton Carrfield, Thurnscoe Hill, Darfield Council
6: Rawmarsh Monkwood, Dearne Highgate
4: Wath Central, Bolton Lacewood, Brampton Ellis, Mexborough St John's
3: Swinton Fitzwilliam
2: Swinton Brookfield, Thurnscoe Gooseacre, Kilnhurst

Both boys and girls are allowed to play in these matches. However, it was not until May 2022 that the organisers staged a girls-only cup to coincide

1925 Totty Cup winners Wath National School

Action from the inaugural Don & Dearne Girls' Cup final between Mexborough St Johns and Brampton Ellis

with the Women's European Championships.

The winners of the inaugural Don & Dearne Girls' Cup were Mexborough St John's who beat Brampton Ellis on penalties.

The Totty Cup will celebrate 100 years with the 2023 final played back where it all began – in Goldthorpe – at the end of March.

Plans are being laid to produce a book to mark the centenary. Anyone who has memories of the Totty Cup is encouraged to share these at tottycup.co.uk

The Barlow-Salmons Shield

Frank Barlow and Geoff Salmons had been coached by the Don & Dearne School Sports Association throughout their schooldays.

Geoff Salmons, born 1948, played for Sheffield United, Stoke City and Leicester City in the First Division, as well as Chesterfield, making almost 500 professional appearances between 1967 and 1981. The winger scored about 50 goals. After a spell with non-League Gainsborough Trinity, Geoff retired to run a pub in Mexborough.

Midfielder Frank Barlow, born 1946, captained the England Schoolboys team. He went on to play more than 260 games

Geoff Salmons, left, and Frank Barlow, right, at Chesterfield

Frank Barlow and Geoff Salmons have been lifelong friends. Here they are in the Swinton Bridge Primary School team in 1957. Frank is sitting with the ball between his feet. Geoff is second from the right on the same row

for Sheffield United and Chesterfield before a brief spell in the USA with Boston Minutemen. However, he made his name as a coach, managing Chesterfield and Scunthorpe United, as well as being caretaker boss at Nottingham Forest and Wigan Athletic. He was also assistant manager at Sheffield United and other coaching roles included Barnsley, Sheffield Wednesday, Birmingham City, Bristol City, Walsall, Hull City and Bradford City.

As a mark of appreciation, Geoff and Frank donated a trophy for those schools knocked out in the early rounds – this is known as the Barlow-Salmons Shield and was introduced in 1974.

Prior to this, there was a Clarke Shield. That was named in memory of Herbert Clarke (secretary of the Don & Dearne Football Association). He was also chairman of English Schools FA in 1966.

For many years, the Barlow-Salmons Shield has been played for by the losing semi-finalists in the Totty Cup – effectively a third place play-off. In 2023, it will revert to being competed for by those schools knocked out of the Totty Cup in the autumn.

In 2024 the Barlow-Salmons Shield will celebrate 50 years. Another publication has been proposed for this too. Anyone who has memories of the Shield is encouraged to share them at *tottycup.co.uk*

Swinton Queen Street, the first Barlow-Salmons Shield winners in 1974. Right, 2022 victors Wath Victoria, with the school's first Don & Dearne trophy since winning the inaugural Totty Cup in 1923

Don & Dearne Schools FA

The Don & Dearne SFA's successful representative teams have produced many professional players.

This was comparable to a football academy of its day and Mark Jones (Manchester United), Gordon West (Everton) and Kevin McHale (Huddersfield Town) are notable graduates from the Don & Dearne Schools FA system.

The association had a special relationship with Sheffield United, providing many players to their junior and reserve teams.

Those who went on to the first team included Tony Wagstaff, Barrie Wagstaff, Steve Goulding, Mick Speight, Ian Holmes and Ken Mallender, as well as Frank Barlow and Geoff Salmons, while Alan Warboys went to Doncaster Rovers.

The 1975 Don & Dearne representative team

Making history – a British Empire Medal for a Mont winner

Barnsley club legend Norman Rimmington was a Mont winner.

Norman, who died in 2016, aged 93, was part of Denaby United's 1955 Mont-winning team, but made his name as a goalkeeper with Hartlepools United between 1947 and 1952. He made 124 appearances for the County Durham coastal side, having earlier appeared 27 times for Barnsley.

Born in Staincross, Norman returned to Yorkshire and Denaby United on his retirement from the professional game. He was then appointed to the coaching staff at Barnsley and stayed at Oakwell until past his 90th birthday, also fulfilling roles as assistant manager, groundsman, chartered physio and kit man. Known as 'Mr Barnsley' and simply 'Rimmo', he was with the club for 70 years.

Norman was awarded a British Empire Medal for services to the local community and football in the 2017 New Year Honours List, being told just days before he passed away. His family received the medal on his behalf.

Norman Rimmington was with Barnsley into his 90s

Subscribers

Bill Adamson
Roy Alford
David Anglesea – Swinton
Ian Appleyard
Chris Atkin
Stephen Bailey – Rawmarsh Welfare, Horse & Jockey
Nick Bainbridge – Worksop
Jamie Ball – Goldthorpe
George Bartholomew – GRB Minerals Ltd
John & Vicki Beal
Ian Beardsley – Swinton WMC FC
Colin Beasley
Bob Bennett – Denaby United
Colin Beverley – Swinton Athletic
Dougie Booth
Giles Brearley
Carl Brennan – Houghton Main
Carl Brown
Tony Buckley
Colin Bullock
Stan Burkinshaw
Albert Burrows, Jennifer Taylor,
   Susan Harrison & Peter Farmery
Joe Byron – Scawthorpe AFC, the Tangerine Army
Dave Cairns – Denaby United, Mexborough Town
Ian Campbell
David Roy Catling
Alan Clamp
Clarky (Mick Clark)
Richard Clayton
Alan Cliff – Goldthorpe Colliery
Andrew Cliff
Frank Cocking (Bowbroom WMC 1951) & Lee Cocking
Terence Collinson – High Terrace
Terry Collinson – High Terrace Football Club
Terry Collinson – Plant Hotel Mexborough
Bill Cook – Swinton Athletic 1972
Dale Cook
Mick Cooke – 2022 referee 125th anniversary final
Paul Cooke – six Montagu Cup finals
Stephen Cooke – Montagu Cup final referee 1992
David Cooper
Gary Cooper
Wilf Cope
Ian Cotton – Mexborough Main Street,
   Swinton Athletic
Dave Cox – referee
Allan Craw – my football hero, Denis Law

Barrie Dalby
Colin Dawson
Ray Dawson
Tracy Dawson
Eric Day
Brian Churchill Dutton – Mexborough Tech Old Boys,
   Runners-up (1956), Winners (1957)
Pete Dyson – High Terrace FC
Walter Earp & Wilfred Booth
David Elliott – Swinton Athletic
Chris Eyre – Rotherham Charity Cup
Michael Fallon
Ian Fareham
Peter Flaherty
Danny Flannery – Sheffield United, Kilnhurst Welfare
Robert Furniss – Westville FC
Eric Gill – Sheffield Wednesday
Martin Gill – Leeds United
Albert Gillott – 1953 Montagu Cup-winning goal
James Glennon
Freddie Goulty
Ronald & Beryl Gray – Denaby United Reserves 1955
George Greenwood – Denaby United,
   Mexborough Main Street
Brian Grime & Janet Howard
Neil Hall – Westward Ho!
Nigel Hanks
The last in line of the John Charles Heatons
Brian Hill – Runners-Up (1956), Winners (1957)
Micky Horne – Mexborough Town, Spalding United
The Horners
Brian "Boe" Hyde – Swinton Athletic & referee
Cat Iles – Dearne CMW, Goldthorpe Colliery
Jackie & Jason – Crown Inn, Barnburgh
   & Harlington Inn
Stephen Jaszczyk
Ron Jevons
Arthur Jones – High Terrace Football Club
Bryn Jones – Mexborough Main Street Club
George Jowett Memorial Trophy
Paul Kay
Kenneth King – Mexborough Tech Old Boys,
   Worksop Town, Denaby Utd, Mexborough Town
Douglas Kirby
Cliff Lacey
Neil Lacey – Parkgate, Goldthorpe Colliery
Bob Lamb – Mexborough Athletic
Thomas (Tommy) Law

Thomas Law
Bill Lawrence
George Laycock
Ken Lee – Mexborough Tech Old Boys
Maxine License
Gary Lindsay – Northgate Club
George Lockwood
John McCall – Mexborough Tech Old Boys
Joe Maloney – Dearne CMW 1982, Goldthorpe Colliery 1990
Gary Mansell
Jordan Mansell
Kevin Manton, Mexborough
Carl Mason – Mexborough Tech Old Boys
Cindy Mason
Ray Mason
Mexborough and District Heritage Society
Peter Miles
Gary Moody
Rodger Mortimer
Kevin Norburn
John Norton – 1978 Montagu Cup final referee
Mike O'Brien
Mel Ogden
Jed O'Neill – Denaby & Cadeby Miners Welfare
Les Oxer – Mexborough Town, Denaby United
Les Payne
John Pearson
Neil Peart – Northcliffe Club FC
Pete Pettit – Mexborough Town, Denaby United
Mick Poole – Montagu Cup final referee 2004 & 2020
Steve Poole – Mexborough Athletic FC
Steve Pugh
Wilf Race
John Ransford – Swinton WMC
Callum, Leila, Isaac and Sienna Richardson
Jon Ripley
Winston Rigg – Denaby United, Tom Hill, Sheffield Wednesday
George Robledo – Totty Cup (1939, 1940), Montagu Cup (1944), World Cup final tournament Brazil (1950), FA Cup (1951/1952)
Geoff Salmons – Sheffield United, Stoke City, Leicester City
Dean Salt
John Salt
Colin Sapey
Harold Sapey – Denaby United, Mexborough Town, Bridlington
In memory of Joseph Sapey
Neil Sigsworth
In memory of Lionel Smith

David Snodgrass
Chris Speight – Mexborough Main Street
Christopher Speight
Howard Spencer – Westville FC
Jimmy Spencer – Mexborough Main Street Club
Dale Spiby
Ken Spiby
Past & present Stelrad employees
Vera Stringer
Gordon Swann
Margaret Swann
Swinton Athletic FC #WASAAW
Michael Takacs
Walter Taylor – Kilnhurst & Parkgate Welfare
Brian Thompson
Alison Toole
Brian Turton – Doncaster Rovers, Scarborough, Swinton Athletic
John David Turton
Joseph Venables (1916-1994) – Winner 1938 Thurnscoe Vics
Kevin Waddle
Tex Walker
Ian Walsh – AM to PM Travel
Cyril Warren 1917-1993
Cyril Warren, Sam Warren, Kenn Warren, David Warren
Glyn (Taffy) Watkin – Tom Hill Old Boys, Kilnhurst Welfare, Denaby United
Stephen Watkin – Denaby & Cadeby Miners Welfare 1989
John Barry Weaver
Martin Weir – Mexborough Main Street
Martyn Weir – Mexborough Main Street
Terry Whitaker
Andrew Whitehead – Swinton Athletic
Barry Whitehead – Mexborough Northgate
Ken Whitehead – Swinton Athletic, Denaby United
Mick Whitehead & Julie Scott-Whitehead
Terry Whitehead
The Whitehouse Family
Dean Whitehouse – Wath Saracens, High Terrace
Ken Whitehouse was a legend
David Whitworth & Walter Aram
Ken Wilkinson
Phil Winfield best wishes Vera
Andy Wordsworth – In memory of GW Wordsworth
Colin Wren – 3 times winner of the Montagu Cup
The Wren Family

Acknowledgments

Thank you to the following for their help in the production of this book. Their assistance and knowledge has been greatly appreciated.

Many others have also assisted and we thank them all for their input. Please forgive us if we have missed anyone out but all contributions are gratefully acknowledged. An updated list of helpers will be available on the *www.montagucup.com* website.

Pete Pettit
Wilf Race
Barrie Dalby
Les Payne
Brian Hill
Allan Craw
Malc Whitehouse
Tim @dribblingcode
Nick Bainbridge
Nigel Burkinshaw
Kenny Harwood
Elizabeth Robledo
Bob Lamb
Mick Swann
Stan Burkinshaw
Jamie Ball
Martin Birley
Steve Poole
Linda Carlton
Dave Kelly
Colin Dawson
Pete Scott
George Frith
Ian Beardsley
Jeff Earnshaw
Sue Everson
Paul Kay
Terry Simon
Paul Hyde
Rob Furniss
Gordon Swann
Andy Billups
Sean Mahon
Ken & Margaret Lee
Clive Newey
Pete Newey
Matty Kelly
Glenn Hancock
Ian Cotton
Dean Beresford
Malcolm Parkinson
Chris Rodgers
Jennifer Taylor
Mark Brennan
Cat Isles
Jan Penny
Jordan Penny
Cyril Skinner
Ian Walsh
Andy Wordsworth
Janet & Mexborough Athletic Club
Clifton Park Archives and Local Studies, Rotherham

Media
Amber Stainrod (Around Town)
David Beddows (Rotherham Advertiser)
Ashley Ball (Barnsley Chronicle)
David Wood (Barnsley FC historian)
Paul Goodwin (Doncaster Free Press)
Paul Claydon (Groundtastic magazine)
Chris O'Keefe (Turnstiles magazine)
Jim Stewart (Football Weekends magazine)

Bibliography
Football in Kilnhurst 1890-1970 by John Howitt
Amateurs Comrades and Primitives by Barry Chambers
England Schoolboys 1907-99 by Gavin Willacy
A Short History of the Montagu Hospital by Donald M Wilson
Soccer at War by Jack Rollin
The Who's Who of Barnsley FC by Grenville Firth & David Wood
From Pit Town to Battlefields by Bill Lawrence
All for the Wolves by Stan Cullis
Football League Players' Records 1888-1939 by Michael Joyce
The PFA Premier and Football League Players' Records 1946-1998 by Barry J Hugman
The FA Cup Complete Results by Tony Brown
An English Football Internationalists' Who's Who by Douglas Lamming
Towering Tales & A Ripping Yarn by Steven Penny

Picture credits

Front cover: Ben Webster (2015), Steve Hall (1988), Steven Penny (2021, cup and plaque), The Western Australia Football Hall of Fame (Pele and Barry Harwood picture), Vanity Fair (Andrew Montagu portrait), South Yorkshire Times and family collections (others).

Back cover: Sean Mahon (Aerial picture)

5 – Professional Darts Corporation/You Tube
11 – Ben Webster (2015) and Kris at Blueline Photography (2020)
14 – Dawson family collection, Kris at Blueline Photography (2020).
15 – Gregg Kerry, Shaun Needham and Ben Webster (2015)
16 – Shaun Flannery (1995) and Tim @dribblingcode
17 – Shaun Flannery (1998) and Tim @dribblingcode
18 – Steve Hall (1988)
20 – Kris at Blueline Photography (2020)
21 – Ben Webster (2015)
22-41 – South Yorkshire Times and family collections
43 – Anne Shaw Simmonite
44–46: South Yorkshire Times
47 – South Yorkshire Times and Chris Eyre
48 – Steve Hall (1988)
49 – Steve Hall (1989) and Shaun Flannery (1994)
50 – Shaun Flannery (1997)
51 – South Yorkshire Times and Liz Robinson (2007)
52 – Holly Allen (2008)
53 – Andrew Roe (2012) and Ben Webster (2015)
54 – Ben Webster (2015)
55 – Ben Webster (2015) and Tim @dribblingcode (2017, 2018)
56 – Steven Penny (2021) and Kris at Blueline Photography (2020)
57 – Mike Bayly (2022) and Tim @dribblingcode (2022)
58 – Mike Bayly (2022) and Julian Barker (2022)
60 – Anonymous and John Hobson (2022)
61 – John Hobson (2022)
63-65 – Family collections
67 – Brian Hill
68 – John Hobson and not known
70, 71 – Robledo family collection
72 – Chris Rodgers
73 – South Yorkshire Times (1986) and Rotherham Advertiser
74 – John Hobson (2022), Tim @dribblingcode (2018) and Kris at Blueline Photography (2021)
78 – Steve Hall (1988, 1991) and Shaun Flannery (1995, 1997)
79 – Jim Reeve
80 – Julian Barker (2022)
81 – Holly Allen (2008)
82 – Steve Hall (1991) and Kris at Blueline Photography (2020, 2021)
83 – Holly Allen (2009) and Andrew Roe (2012)
85 – Ben Webster (2015), Julian Barker and Dave Poucher/Rotherham Advertiser
86 – Vanity Fair (Andrew Montagu portrait)
87 – South Yorkshire Times
89 – Andrew Roe (2012), Kris at Blueline Photography (2021), Shaun Flannery (1994), John Hobson (2022) and South Yorkshire Times (1976, 1993)
90 – Mike Bayly (2022)
92 – Kris at Blueline Photography (2020)
93 – South Yorkshire Times
96 – South Yorkshire Times
97 – Dawson family collection
98 – Published under Creative Commons 2.0 licence
100-108 – Kris at Blueline Photography (2020, 2021) and Nick Bainbridge (2022)
110 – Steven Penny (2021) and Kris at Blueline Photography (2021)
111, 112 – Dave Poucher/Rotherham Advertiser
113 – Yorkshire Post (Norman Rimmington)
119 – The Western Australia Football Hall of Fame

Thanks go to JPI Media for their kind permission to use pictures from the South Yorkshire Times (and associated titles, including the Yorkshire Post, Sheffield Star and Doncaster Free Press).

Unless stated, pictures are from the South Yorkshire Times, family collections or an unknown source.

Many pictures have been submitted from private family collections and details of the original photographer are not known. Some donors have asked to remain anonymous.

Every effort has been made to acknowledge the source of specific illustrations and photographers where they are known and to ensure copyright has not been infringed. We apologise if you believe your work has been used without permission. If this is the case, contact the publisher in the first instance.

BOOKSHELF

Long-standing non-League football writer Steve Penny has had a busy few months, putting together no fewer than five new books, including the one you are holding – The Mont, 125 years of the Mexborough Montagu Hospital Charity Cup, 1897-2022.

The Tyke Travels yearbook author went back to basics during the tail end of the Covid lockdown to produce a book about grassroots football in Yorkshire, discovering many links to the very pinnacle of the game with visits to 31 grounds across the Broad Acres.

Towering Tales & A Ripping Yarn is £11.99 from Amazon – tinyurl.com/ToweringTales
(Also available as an ebook at £9.99)

He followed that up with a long weekend in Lisbon to produce 'Tarts, Trams & Tuk Tuks', which according to the *portugoal.net* website is: "A little gem of a book depicting the adventures (and misadventures) of a group of English football tourists on a long weekend trip to Lisbon. Written in a lively, entertaining and informative style… the perfect appetiser for anyone intending to visit Lisbon to take in the football and non-football experiences the Portuguese capital has to offer."

Tarts, Trams & Tuk Tuks is £6 (plus £1.65 postage) via eBay – tinyurl.com/eBayTuks

Steve was off on his travels again to catch some winter sun and returned from Lanzarote with a fascinating account of football on the Canary Island. Island Hopping features every club on the island, with detailed visitor guide, an account of his trip and the history of the sport on Lanzarote.

Island Hopping – the football grounds of Lanzarote is £14.99 and available from Amazon – tinyurl.com/LanzGrounds

Finally, a bit closer to home, Steve spent a lot of time traversing the highways and byroads of Lincolnshire to compile the first complete guide to football in the county.
Pilgrims' Patch covers all 160-plus teams in Lincolnshire, from Football League to parks football with a comprehensive history section, courtesy of Martyn Girdham.
The full-colour book has sections on all 'Pyramid' clubs, with fantastic ground pictures, travel details, kits and club badges.

Pilgrims' Patch – the football grounds of Lincolnshire is £15.99 and also available from Amazon – tinyurl.com/LincsPatch

Penny for your Sports Publications – Steve Penny Media – tinyurl.com/spennymedia

Final whistle

Making it big Down Under

Kenny Boden was not the only man from Mont territory who made it big Down Under (see Page 63). Barry Harwood also went on to appear on Australia's biggest stage and even shared a pitch with Pele.

Barry played in the Montagu Cup for Swinton Athletic before becoming a referee and it was as a man in black that he made his name after emigrating.

He officiated in four full internationals, blowing his whistle for his adopted nation in their 3-0 defeat to the USSR in Adelaide in 1975, a 1-1 draw against Israel in Melbourne in 1977 and at the same venue, three years later, when he oversaw a 2-2 draw for the Socceroos against a Czechoslovakia side that included Antonin Panenka, of cheeky penalty kick fame.

His final international honour came in 1988 when he refereed a 2-2 draw between Argentina and Saudi Arabia in Adelaide. It was in that last match that he rubbed shoulders with the legendary Pele, who was the celebrity guest for the pre-match coin toss.

As well as international fixtures, Barry also took charge of matches between Australian sides and visiting teams from the United Kingdom. Among them were Aberdeen and Chelsea (1974), Manchester United and Rangers (1975), Tottenham and Sunderland (1976), Middlesbrough (1977), Dundee (1978), Nottingham Forest (1984), Tottenham again (1985) and Millwall (1989).

When the World Youth Championships were

Barry with Pele in 1988 and, right, in more recent times

held in Australia in 1981, Barry showed some of the world's top officials a clean pair of heels in the fitness test, being declared FIFA's fittest referee, when he covered 3,400 metres in a 12-minute run.

It was all a far cry from his early days at Kilnhurst CofE Primary School and Rawmarsh Haugh Road Secondary School. He captained Rotherham Schoolboys and was offered apprenticeships at Rotherham United and Doncaster Rovers but his parents insisted he got a 'proper' job. However, Barry did turn out for Rotherham United's u18s Northern Intermediate team, as well as Swinton Athletic and Denaby United.

He took his Sheffield & Hallamshire County FA referees exam in 1963, advancing to Grade 1 by 1966, when he moved to Perth, Western Australia. Within two years he was the man in the middle for inter-state matches and in 1969 refereed Western Australia's encounter with Greece. He was referee for the visit of Lev Yashin's Moscow Dynamo team in 1970 and two years later earned a place on the FIFA list. That brought foreign travel and he officiated at matches in Indonesia, Canada, Thailand, Singapore, Taiwan and New Zealand, as well as refereeing the final of the 1989 Oceania Women's Soccer Tournament. *(continued overleaf)*

Barry (standing, fifth from left) with the successful Swinton Athletic team of 1962

Barry took charge of matches featuring British touring teams in Australia, shaking hands with captains including: Stuart Boam, Martin O'Neill, Frank Munro, Steve Perryman and Sammy McIlroy

Barry was named Western Australia's Soccer Sportsman of the Year in 1980 and, five years after retiring, was inducted into the Western Australia Hall of Recognition for Soccer.

As a result of his achievements with the whistle, Barry was given the honour of carrying the Olympic Torch when the Games came to Sydney in 2000.

After 54 years in Australia, Barry moved to Nagoya in Japan in 2020, after donating seven boxes of memorabilia, including his much-valued FIFA blazer, for use in the Western Australian Football Museum, which is due to open in 2023.

Several years after appearing in the Mont as a player, Barry returned as a referee, taking charge of a potentially explosive quarter-final clash between Conisbrough Northcliffe and Mexborough Town.

Former Rotherham Advertiser and Sheffield Star journalist Les Payne takes up the tale: "In 1977 Barry was visiting the UK over the festive period and the feisty clash was due to take place on New Year's Eve on the top field above Denaby United. Northcliffe were threatening to do all sorts to Mexborough so someone decided to get Barry to referee the match.

"I was at that game and Northcliffe fancied they could bully Mexborough out of it. But they got it back big time from Mexborough who scored twice early on and won 4-0 in a game brilliantly refereed."

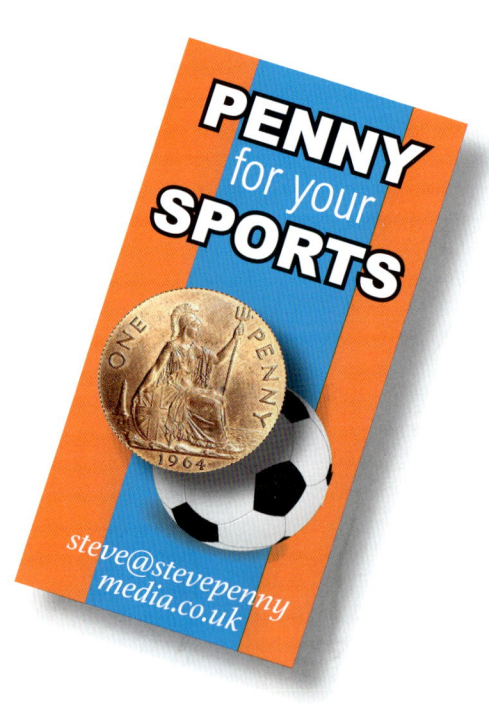